pretty little things to MAKE

pretty little things to MAKE

20 Heirloom Projects for Babies and Toddlers

JUDITH MORE

COLLINS & BROWN

To the memory of my mother, Audrey

First published in the United Kingdom in 2009
by Collins & Brown
10 Southcombe Street, London W14 0RA

An imprint of Anova Books Company Ltd

Copyright © Fil Rouge Press Ltd 2009

Distributed in the United States and Canada
by Sterling Publishing Co,
387 Park Avenue South, New York,
NY 10016-8810, USA

The moral right of the author has been
asserted.

ISBN 978-1-84340-504-7

A CIP catalogue for this book is available
from the British Library.

10 9 8 7 6 5 4 3 2 1

For Fil Rouge Press
Publisher: Judith More
Editor: Jo Godfrey Wood
Designer: Janis Utton
Photographer: Robin Lever

Reproduction by Rival Colour Ltd, UK
Printed and bound by [Printer]

This book can be ordered direct from the
publisher.

Contact the marketing department,
but try your bookshop first.

www.anovabooks.com

Contents

Introduction

The purpose of this little book is to help you make exquisite things from times gone by, so that you can create treasured heirlooms for tomorrow. Vintage baby and toddler clothes can be adorable, but inevitably that special piece you track down is never exactly the right size, or never quite launders to the freshness you want. So making new vintage-inspired things is the perfect way to enjoy nostalgic fashion and gives you the pleasure of making them, too.

Ever since I was a teenager, I have been collecting vintage clothing, sewing and knitting patterns. I have found things in charity shops in Devon, England, yard sales in Washington DC and flea markets in France. More recently online auctions have widened my net to as far away as Australia. Now classic designs for children are becoming fashionable again and since I don't have any little ones of my own, I decided it was time to share some highlights from the kids' section of my collection with those of you who do.

Scattered alongside photographs of pretty little things wearing or using the projects are some charming vintage illustrations to set the mood, or even inspire you to create your own

Pretty hearts The 1950s cotton dress, right, was found unworn in a dusty shop stockroom.

Daisy chain Make a perfect summer's day tiara or necklace out of real daisies by splitting stalks and threading through.

adaptations. As well as the projects, there's extra advice that helps you make the most of your work. For example, party-lovers will find ideas for holding a vintage-style baby shower and for wrapping gifts, and inventive children's fancy-dress suggestions from times gone by. While at the end of the book a practical primer supports the project instructions, looks at using vintage fabrics, buttons and ribbons and advises on using old tools and sewing machines.

To make up the projects, I've chosen natural fabrics and yarns that match, or are in sympathy with, the materials used in the original designs. I also give some advice on recycling vintage household linens for a simple and inexpensive way to make cute little clothes. It's often easy to track these items down in boot sales and charity shops. Using these linens can create a charming link between the generations – you can turn the embroidered tablecloth great-grandma stitched at school into a pretty pinafore for her great-grand-daughter's baking sessions. And repurposing beautiful old fabrics, rather than throwing them away and buying new, is excellent for the environment, too.

Some projects have been created especially for this book. For example, I had a craving for a Candy Cane Christmas Stocking, but I couldn't find an old design that matched my imaginary festive knit, so I dug out a century-old bedsock pattern and reinvented it for a twenty-first-century Christmas by adding a candy-cane effect and knitting it up in an ultra-chunky wool. The finished result was as good as a sugar-high – so I'd strongly encourage you to try your hand at adapting vintage patterns as a gentle path into designing your own.

Reworking vintage designs for kids to wear today is often a great deal easier than hunting for a rare original. And even if you find one ready-made, it is best not to attempt to make an authentic head-to-toe outfit unless the end result is to be worn at a fancy dress party or a school

French chic This exquisite soft muslin antique
dress is punctuated with borders and rondels of
firm French knots.

Sweetest smocking An ancient form of decoration, smocking was extensively used on children's clothes in the C20th.

handed down to my younger sister, it was so out of fashion that she was teased mercilessly. She came home from one party in a terrible rage, sneaked some scissors out of the kitchen and cut it into little pieces. So before you fill up your toddler's closet with old-fashioned charm, make sure that your child buys into your vintage taste.

The final versions and instructions provided in this book don't slavishly follow the old designs. They have been updated to meet today's needs, skill sets and style ideas (and so are unlikely to fall victim to a teased toddler out for revenge). Many of the projects are easy enough for beginners, but if they are a tad more difficult or time-consuming to put together I've supplied 'cheat's' suggestions to give you simpler alternatives or short-cuts for a fast result: you'll want to finish the project before your child grows too big to wear or use it. Whether you want to make a gift for a friend's baby shower, christening or naming ceremony, or you are a mother or grandmother wanting to create a special something for the newest member of your family, you can happily take up your knitting needles or set up your sewing machine and enjoy creating your own pretty little heirloom.

stage production. Try mixing vintage treasures with modern things to create a really stylish, up-to-date result. The same applies to the designs in this book. For example, the boy's Striped Sweater on page 76 was originally designed to go with matching knitted shorts, but your child will probably feel much happier in a pair of ordinary denim cut-offs.

Bear in mind that even small children are extremely fashion-conscious. By the time my favourite poodle-printed party dress, which I wore enthusiastically, was

Sailor suited A special find from the 1930s in white linen, this sailor top came as a set with front-buttoned bell bottoms.

Baby Shower

Handmade presents show your expectant friends and brand-new mums just how much you care, and your efforts will be treasured for years to come. Who could possibly sneeze at a charming **achoo stroller quilt** or pass on **ABC jeanius blocks**? Every mum and baby will fall in love with the floppiest **skinny monkey**, and you'll adore knitting the new arrival box-fresh **snowdrop bootees** in milk cotton yarn. The chapter finishes with gift-wrapping ideas focusing on a **stork** theme.

Achoo Stroller Quilt

The quirky designs on vintage printed cotton handkerchiefs make perfect blocks for the top of a patchwork stroller quilt. If you don't have a stock of laundered gems in the family linen closet, then look for modern versions that have a nostalgic feel. The original purpose of hankies hasn't been overlooked: I designed this quilt with a secret pocket in the central patch to take an extra hankie or a few tissues that your little one can actually use.

FINISHED SIZE
56 x 82 cm/22 x 32 in.

LEVEL
Easy. Skills required: machine-seam; top-stitching.

MATERIALS
5 vintage printed cotton handkerchiefs, each approximately 21 cm/8$^{1}/_{2}$ in square

1.8 m/2 yd cotton fabric in the colour of your choice for the quilt ground

1 m/1 yd ready-quilted batting for the quilt backing

Cotton thread in the colour of the ground fabric

HOW TO CHEAT
If you're running short of time and need to make the quilt in a hurry, perhaps as a present, try cutting a few corners. The ready-finished edges on purchased hankies mean that you can simply no-sew appliqué them onto the top of a ready-made plain stroller quilt using fusible webbing. Cut squares of webbing to the same size as the hankies, then position each hankie and webbing sandwich on the quilt top and iron in place.

A true pocket hankie One upper side of the central diamond-placed patch is left unstitched to provide a secret pocket for a useful handkerchief.

METHOD

1 To make the quilt top, cut out a rectangle of ground fabric 91 cm x 66 cm/36 in x 26 in or sized to suit you.

2 Arrange your hankies on the quilt top, spacing them evenly or you can space them more randomly. You can use the gingham pattern as a guide to get the effect you want. Allow an additional 5 cm/2 in seam allowance around the four sides of the quilt.

3 Using the thread colour of your choice – matching or contrasting, it's up to you, and working just inside the hanky hems,

top-stitch them in place, leaving one or both edges of the central hankie free, so that you can make a secret hankie pocket or two.

4 Cut batting backing fabric to the same size as the quilt top. With the wrong sides together either pin or tack the batting to the quilt top.

5 Allowing a 5 cm/2 in seam allowance, machine-stitch around three sides.

6 Turn. Fold in edges and top-stitch the open end closed.

Oh sew easy! A set of unused vintage hankies
are simple to place accurately on a gingham
ground for a vintage-style twist on a colourful
patchwork quilt.

ABC Jeanius Blocks

A nineteenth-century German embroidery alphabet was the starting point for designing the letters on these blocks. You'll find the charts for the vintage alphabet I used on page 21; all 26 letters are there, so you can make a whole alphabet. Otherwise, just pick a suitable word or phrase, or work the letters of the baby's name. I decided that cross-stitch would look good on a tough denim recycled from old jeans. If you have kept old jeans, this is an Earth- and purse-friendly recycling project.

FINISHED SIZE
Per block: 8 cm/3¼ in square.

LEVEL
Easy. Skills required: Simple machine-seam; slip-stitch; cross-stitch (see page 125).

MATERIALS
Recycled denim scraps or a length of new denim: 1 m/1 yd makes 6 blocks
Toy filling (purchased approved stuffing)
Heavy-duty blue cotton thread
Embroidery thread in chosen colours
Embroidery needle
Denim needle for your sewing machine

HOW TO CHEAT
Hate embroidery? Then cut out block pieces as described in Step 1 of the Method. Omit Step 2 and instead photocopy the letter pattern and trace it onto the paper side of fusible webbing. Place the fusible sheet wrong side down on primary-coloured gingham fabric and press, following manufacturer's instructions. Cut out the appliqué letter, remove the paper backing and press onto a square. Follow Steps 2 to 8 to make up the block.

Cross-stitch blocks Use traditional cross-stitch letters to spell out a special message or your child's name.

METHOD

1 To make one block, cut out six 10 cm/4 in squares from denim.

2 Following the chart on the facing page, embroider the letter centrally on one square of denim.

3 With right sides together, and a 1.5 cm/½ in seam allowance, seam four of the plain squares together to form a lengthwise strip.

4 Next, sew the beginning of the strip to the end of the strip, with right sides facing, so that you eventually form an open cube.

5 With right side facing down into the cube, seam the letter square to the top of the open cube, pivoting at corners.

6 Sew the last square to the bottom of the cube, right side facing in, leaving an opening for stuffing on one side.

7 Using an approved toy stuffing (suitable for toys, with a CE mark), fill the cube until it is firm and looks square.

8 Slip-stitch the opening closed.

Repeat Steps 1 to 8 to make as many blocks as you like.

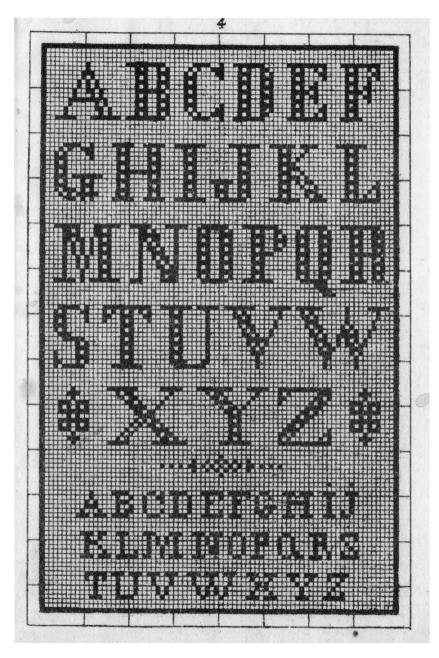

Vintage cross-stitch chart An alphabet that
dates from the C19th, used as a basis for the
blocks shown left.

Skinny Monkey

As a child, I was in love with my wonderful velveteen monkey. He had a wire skeleton buried in his stuffing, so I would bend his hand around the back of my chair and he'd hang there, as though he was in a tree. The monkey shown here, based on a darling 1920s French design, is more of a softie. Today, we are more aware of the dangers of wires that could poke through and harm the child, so do not use them. Today's child won't miss the monkey's skeleton, though, and will adore a floppy friend who can bend and twist any which way.

FINISHED SIZE

The monkey is 60 cm/23½ in tall (big enough for a tot to hug).

LEVEL

Intermediate. Skills required: machine-seam; chain-stitch, satin-stitch.

MATERIALS

1 yd/1 m of brown fabric (I used cotton moleskin)
Small piece of beige felt
Toy filling
Embroidery thread in brown and rose pink
Sewing thread in brown
Ribbon remnant

METHOD

1 Photocopy and enlarge the pattern from page 129.

2 With the right sides placed together, fold the main fabric in half lengthways (so that the pile on the back and the front goes in the same direction), and pin the body pattern, the pattern that forms the top and back of the head, and the tail pattern in place. Cut out.

3 Cut out the face and ears from beige felt, using the pattern pieces provided.

4 With right sides together, sew around the body, following the 1 cm/3/8 in seam

allowance and leaving the neck and last 4 cm/1 1/2 in of arms and legs open (as marked on the pattern).

5 Working from the neck opening, turn the body right sides out.

6 Add the toy filling (again via the neck opening), starting with the arms, then the legs. Take care not to overstuff the arms and legs, or they won't be flexible enough. Stuff the body firmly.

7 Finish the hands and feet off with four embroidered lines of slip-stitch, stitched through both layers of fabric, to indicate the monkey's fingers and toes. Fold in the seam allowance, press. Finally hand-sew the side seams of the toy's hands and feet closed.

8 Start assembling the head. With the first head piece folded in half, right sides together, insert one folded felt ear at the top of the seam and stitch in place. Repeat with the second piece and ear. Pin the two head pieces together, right sides facing.

9 Sew the beige felt face piece to the head pieces. Clip the seams, to ease.

10 Finally, with the wrong sides together, join the marked seam on the head pieces, to form the top of the head. Clip the seam as marked, to ease.

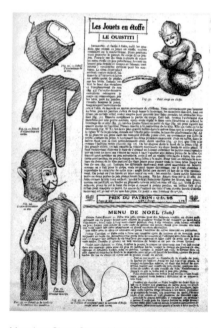

Monsieur Singe Skinny Monkey was inspired by this design in a 1920s craft newsletter.

A soft touch The original design called for brown velvet or fur fabric, but plush moleskin, or even cotton jersey, is just as soft and is much easier to work.

11 Following the photographs for reference, embroider the eyebrows in dark brown, the eyes in black, and the lips and nostrils in dark pinky-red thread. The eyes are worked in a satin filling-stitch (do not use the traditional button eyes as they can be chewed off and swallowed).

12 With right sides together, fold the tail piece in half and seam. Turn right sides out (you may need to use a loop-turner to help you do this) and slip-stitch firmly to the centre back of the monkey (make sure that this is very secure so that the tail cannot be pulled off during over-enthusiastic play).

13 Insert toy filling, then firmly sew the head to the body.

14 Wrap a ribbon collar around the monkey's neck to hide the join, sewing it securely at the back of the neck for safety (a loose ribbon can be a choking hazard).

Snowdrop Bootees

What are bootees but tiny shoes, and what woman with a shoe obsession

can do anything but love tiny, tiny shoes? When an auction-won collection of

vintage bootee patterns from Australia arrived, they were all so dinky I couldn't

decide which designs to rework first. The same day I discovered a delicious

new milk cotton yarn in a warm-white hue called 'Snow' at my favourite

knitting store. I couldn't ignore the serendipity, as the original version of this

design is called Snowdrop.

FINISHED SIZE

Fits a baby from birth to six months.

LEVEL

Intermediate. Skills required: stocking-
stitch, garter-stitch, slip-stitch, increasing,
decreasing, knitting in two colours,
short rows.

MATERIALS

50 g/1¼ oz Rowan Fine Milk Cotton,
    shade 484 Humbugs (soft blue) or
    482 Apple Pips (soft green) or 483
    Shrimps (soft pink)
50 g/1¼ oz Rowan Fine Milk Cotton,
    shade 493 Snow (white)
Note: If the colours are reversed, you will
be able to make two more sets of
bootees from these two balls.
Length of ribbon
2.5 mm needles

GAUGE/TENSION

30 stitches and 38 rows over 10 cm/4 in
stocking stitch.

METHOD

Sole (knit two the same)

Using blue yarn, cast on 8 stitches.

1st row Knit.

2nd row Knit.

3rd row Inc. once into 1st st; K. to last 2 st, inc once in next st, K1 (10 sts).

Continue in garter-st. until work measures 9 cm/3^1/$_2$in.

Next row: K. 2 tog, K. 8, K. 2 tog.

Next row: K.

Cast off.

Top

Using blue yarn, cast on 20 stitches.

1st row Using white yarn, K. 8; turn.

Note: When turning, always bring yarn to front of work, slip first stitch on left-hand needle onto right-hand needle, take yarn to back of work and slip-stitch back onto left-hand needle. Turn, and proceed as given in instructions.

2nd row Using white yarn, P.

3rd row Using blue yarn, K.

4th row Using blue yarn, K.

5th row Using white yarn, K. 8; turn.

6th row Using white yarn, P.

7th row Using blue yarn, K.10, yarn fwd, K.2 tog, K.8.

8th row Using blue yarn, K.

9th row Using white yarn, K. 8; turn.

10th row Using white yarn, P.

11th row Using blue yarn, K.

12th row Using blue yarn, K.

13th row Using white yarn, K. 8; turn.

14th row Using white yarn, P.

15th row Using blue yarn, K.

16th row Using blue yarn, K.

17th row Using white yarn, K. 8; turn.

18th row Using white yarn, P.

19th row Using blue yarn, K.10, yarn fwd, K.2 tog, K.8.

20th row Using blue yarn, K.

21st row Using white yarn, K. 8; turn.

22nd row Using white yarn, P.

23rd row Using blue yarn, K.

24th row Using blue yarn, K.

25th row Using white yarn, K. 8; turn.

26th row Using white yarn, P.

27th row Using blue yarn, K.

28th row Using blue yarn, K.

29th row Using white yarn, K. 8; turn.

30th row Using white yarn, P.

31st row Using blue yarn, K.10, yarn fwd, K.2 tog, K.8.

32nd row Using blue yarn, K.

33rd row Using blue yarn, K.

34th row Using white yarn, inc. 1; K. 8; turn.

35th row Using white yarn, P.

36th row Using blue yarn, K.

37th row Using blue yarn, K.

38th row Using white yarn, inc. 1; K. 9; turn.

39th row Using white yarn, P.

40th row Using blue yarn, K.10, yarn fwd, K.2 tog, K.8.

41st row Using blue yarn, K.

42nd row Using blue yarn, K.

43rd row Using white yarn, inc. 1; K. 10; turn.

Vintage pattern A delightful example from my extensive collection. The original called for a 2-ply pure wool. I have reworked the snowdrop design for today in a sister company's natural fibre, easy-to-wash milk yarn.

56th row Using white yarn, inc. 1; K.13; turn.

57th row Using white yarn, P.

58th row Using blue yarn, K.14, yarn fwd, K.2 tog, K.8.

59th row Using blue yarn, K.

60th row Using white yarn, K. 14; turn.

61st row Using white yarn, P.

62nd row Using blue yarn, K.

63rd row Using blue yarn, K.

64th row Using white yarn, K. 8; turn.

65th row Using white yarn, P.

66th row Using blue yarn, K.15, yarn fwd, K.2 tog, K.8.

67th row Using blue yarn, K.

68th row Using white yarn, K. 14; turn.

69th row Using white yarn, P.

70th row Using blue yarn, K.

71st row Using blue yarn, K.

72nd row Using white yarn, K. 14; turn.

73rd row Using white yarn, P.

74th row Using blue yarn, K.15, yarn fwd, K.2 tog, K.8.

75th row Using blue yarn, K.

76th row Using white yarn, K. 2 tog; K 12; turn.

77th row Using white yarn, P.

78th row Using blue yarn, K.

79th row Using blue yarn, K.

80th row Using white yarn, K. 2 tog; K11; turn.

81st row Using white yarn, P.

82nd row Using blue yarn, K.12, yarn fwd, K.2 tog, K.10.

83rd row Using blue yarn, K.

84th row Using white yarn, K.2 tog; K.10; turn.

Ribbon ties I chose cotton sateen ribbon for its pearly matt sheen. Make sure you sew the ribbon firmly in place at the back, for safety's sake.

44th row Using white yarn, P.

45th row Using blue yarn, K.

46th row Using blue yarn, K.

47th row Using white yarn, inc. 1; K. 11; turn.

48th row Using white yarn, P.

49th row Using blue yarn, K.14, yarn fwd, K.2 tog, K.8.

50th row Using blue yarn, K.

51st row Using blue yarn, K.

52nd row Using white yarn, inc. 1; K. 12; turn.

53rd row Using white yarn, P.

54th row Using blue yarn, K.

55th row Using blue yarn, K.

85th row Using white yarn, P.
86th row Using blue yarn, K.
87th row Using blue yarn, K.
88th row Using white yarn, K. 2 tog.; K9; turn.
89th row Using white yarn, P.
90th row Using blue yarn, K.11, yarn fwd, K.2 tog, K.8.
91st row Using blue yarn, K.
92nd row Using white yarn, K.2 tog; K. 8; turn.
93rd row Using white yarn, P.
94th row Using blue yarn, K.
95th row Using blue yarn, K.

Repeat rows 9-32 once.

119th row Using white yarn, K. 8; turn.

120th row Using white yarn, P.
121st row Using blue yarn, K.
122nd row Using blue yarn, K.
123rd row Using white yarn, K. 8; turn.
124th row Using white yarn, P.
125th row Using blue yarn, cast off.

Work a second bootee to the same instructions.

To finish:
Stitch the back seam of the upper, then the upper to the sole, starting at centre back and working around. Thread the ribbon through the worked holes, matching lengths, and sew firmly at centre back (don't leave the ribbon loose as it is a potential choking hazard).

Newly minted If you are knitting for a baby yet to be born, pale green is a traditional choice if you don't know whether the stork is bringing a boy or a girl.

The Gift of the Stork

A symbol of good fortune and fertility all around the world, the graceful white stork is faithful to its partner and its nest (the Hebrew word for stork translates as 'good mother'). Because the stork is a migratory bird it is associated with spring and new life, like other baby symbols such as lambs, bunnies, chicks and daffodils.

ENTERTAINING MR STORK

The traditional story of the stork delivering the baby to its new family is a charming theme for a vintage-inspired baby shower. The stork is such a popular icon when celebrating the announcement of a new baby that in some countries a baby shower is known as a 'stork party'. Look out for stork-shaped cake tins and cookie (biscuit) cutters to bake treats for shower guests. You can find everything you need embellished with storks, from disposable tableware to swizzle sticks for your non-alcoholic cocktails.

Birth
Announcement.
A little One
has come to.
make our. .
home a . . .
permanent . .
abode . It
is a *boy*.

6382

You've got male! A vintage postcard from 1910 spreads the news of a new arrival.

STORK 'BUNDLE' GIFTWRAP

Create an Earth-friendly bundle in which to present your gift: wrap your present in an old-fashioned terry nappy, and fasten it with a diaper pin (even if your expectant friend intends to use disposables, the terry will come in handy for mopping up baby spills). If you don't like white towelling, try out a pastel-coloured one instead: the traditional blue for boys and pink for girls, perhaps. Complete the effect with a stork-stamped gift tag.

STORK STITCHES

Traditional stork-shaped scissors are pretty to use for sewing and are usually found in a small embroidery size. The story goes that midwives used their blunt needlework scissors for clamping the umbilical cord and the sharp ones for cutting it, and that this practice inspired the shape.

Home-made stork tag Create original gift tags using vintage-print blocks or modern vintage-style stamps. Press them into a coloured ink, then print onto a luggage label, next to the tie. Add your own greeting.

Special Occasions

Garments for little ones stitched by mothers and grandmothers have been at the centre of celebrations such as christenings, weddings and festivals since sewing was invented. Whether it's for a name-day ceremony or christening, gussy up a new baby in a silky **heirloom gown**, then enfold them in the softest **lacy shawl** to share the joy of their birth with family and friends. For toddlers, sew up a crisp **little boy blue shirt** for a pageboy or craft pink ribbon into the sweetest little round **rosy purse** for a bridesmaid or party outing.

Heirloom Gown

A century of babies could have sported the vintage gown shown here. A soft ivory silk and lace confection, it has been lovingly stored and looks as good as new. If you don't have a family hand-me-down, why not make your own heirloom for generations to come. An extra advantage is that your baby's gown can be tailored to fit, as vintage versions are often tiny.

FINISHED SIZE

Length 70 cm/28 in; chest 51 cm/20 in. To fit a three-month-old baby.

LEVEL

Intermediate. Skills required: machine-seam, gathering, top-stitching, French seam, insertion, double-hemming.

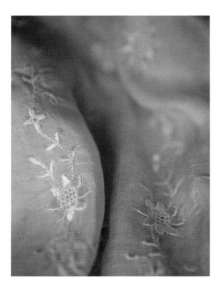

MATERIALS

2 m/2 yd silk or cotton lawn with an embroidered repeat
Matching silk thread
1 m x 1 cm-/1 yd x $3/8$ in-wide lace edging trim
20 cm x 3cm-/8 in x 1$1/4$ in-wide insertion lace
3 invisible press studs

HOW TO CHEAT

Guess what? The original dressmaker cheated; this vintage gown was created from a ready-embroidered silk. Even in the 1920s, when this was made, mothers didn't always hand-embroider their work because commercial machine embroidery had been introduced half a century before, in the 1870s. To get the same effect, choose a fabric with a repeat embroidered motif and a plain section. With a prettily scalloped-edged cotton, you don't even have to hem.

Lace luxe Panels of machine lace set between silk highlight the machine-embroidered motif, adding to the glamour.

METHOD

1 For the skirt, cut a rectangle 75 cm/30 in across and to your required length, making sure that the embroidery on your chosen fabric falls where you need it.

2 For the front yoke cut two pieces 14 cm/5½ in long and 8 cm/3½ in wide and one piece 14 cm/5½ in long and 14 cm/5½ in wide, selecting the embroidered areas you want to feature on the yoke.

3 Cut out two 60 cm/23½ in strips, four 16 cm/6½ in strips and two 35 cm-/14 in-long strips, all 1 cm/½ in wide, from the remaining plain areas. These will serve

as the waistband, sleeve bands and neckbands of the gown.

4 With right sides together, stitch the central back seam, leaving the top 12 cm/4½ in open. Press.

5 Working 2.5 cm/1 in below the raw edge, gather the skirt top. Once gathered, the top of the skirt should measure 51 cm/20 in.

6 Assemble the front yoke. Fold in 1 cm/½ cm seam allowances on inner sides of two outer yoke pieces and outer side edges of the central panel. Press.

7 Place a strip of insertion lace 9 cm/3½ in long between the outer yoke piece and the central yoke panel, on the right side of the fabric, and top-stitch in place. Repeat on the other side of the central panel.

8 Take the assembled front yoke and the two back yoke pieces and, with right sides together, sew the shoulder seams, joining the two back yoke pieces to the front yoke.

9 Press in the seam allowances on the neckbands. Gently easing around the curve, pin the neckbands in place on the right and wrong sides of the yoke, sandwiching the raw edge of the yoke and the bottom of the lace edging between the two bands. Top-stitch in place. Press.

10 Press in the seam allowances on the sleeve bands. Pin the bands in place on the bottom edges of the sleeves, sandwiching the raw edge of the sleeve and the bottom of the lace edging between the two bands. Top-stitch in place. Press.

11 With the right sides of the fabric together, stitch the side seams on the two sleeves. Press.

12 Set in the sleeves, using a French seam (see page 122).

13 Pin the two waistband strips to the bottom of the yoke and the top of the skirt, one on the right side and one on the wrong side, trapping the raw edges between the two bands so that they are concealed. Top-stitch the waistband strips in place.

14 Hem the raw edges of the back opening. Attach the press studs to the back yoke (the original gown closed with gathered ties, but these are considered a choking hazard today).

15 For the hem, fold 6 cm/2¼ in of the bottom of the skirt over twice. Slip-stitch and press.

Size me up Vintage gowns can be tiny, so crafting your own means you can get the right size for your bouncing C21st babe.

Lacy Shawl

Pretty wrappings in pillow-soft yarn are the baby equivalent of a pashmina. The light-as-a-feather spider's web lace patterns of the past are the stuff of dreams, but they do call for advanced skills and time on your hands. If you are a new parent, you'll have more pressing demands on your energies, and today grandmothers have careers, so knitting time is often too short to tackle a complex project. So I have reworked a simple 1930s shawl pattern in a luxurious double-knit yarn. Pamper yourself and your baby or grandchild with an easy design in pure fibres. It still has a hint of traditional lace – the simple openwork border gives an effortless lacy effect.

FINISHED SIZE
137 cm/54 in square.

LEVEL
Extra easy. Skills required: Knit, slip-stitch.

MATERIALS
12 balls Rowan Wool and Cotton, shade 900 Antique
Size 3.75 mm very long knitting needles

GAUGE/TENSION
23 stitches and 18 rows to 10 cm/4 in over garter stitch.

HOW TO CHEAT
The original shawl pattern called for a 4-ply wool and cotton blend. Today's wool and cotton is double-knit, so your shawl will knit up faster. Unlike lace designs, the simple openwork pattern won't suffer from being knitted up in a heavier weight.

METHOD

Cast on 341 stitches.

Rows 1–28 K (garter stitch).

29th row K22 m*1, K2 tog, K3, repeat from * until 24 sts remain, m1, K2 tog, K22.

30th row K23, * m1, K2 tog, K3, repeat from * until 23 sts remain, m1, K2 tog, K21.

Repeat the last 2 rows 20 times.

71st row K 22* m1, K2 tog, K3*, repeat from * to * 5 times, m1, K2 tog, K until 54 sts remain, repeat from * to * 6 times, m1, K2 tog, K22.

72nd row K23, *m1, K2 tog, K3,* repeat from * to * 5 times, m1, K2 tog, K until 53 sts remain, repeat from * to * 6 times, , m1, k2 tog, K21.

Repeat last 2 rows 145 times.

Repeat 29th and 30th rows 21 times.

K 28 rows (garter stitch). Cast off.

To block: Pin out the shawl to measurement (see finished size) and press on the wrong side, using a steam iron.

Size me down To narrow the width, simply reduce the number of stitches you cast on, to make the central panel smaller.

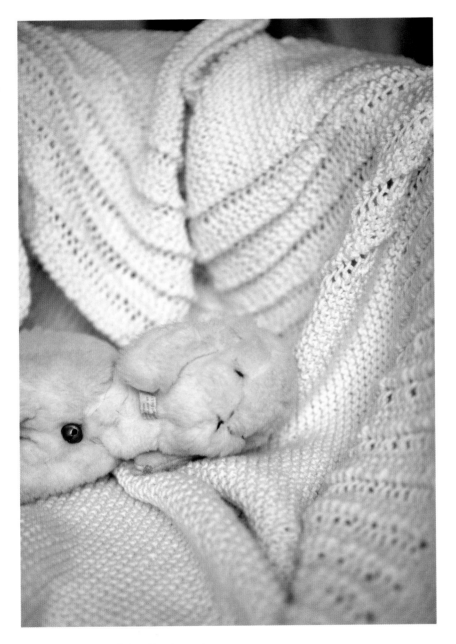

Pure wool and cotton Soft and luxurious, yet
strong, this classic yarn blend is ideal for an
heirloom knit that could enfold generations of
babies to come.

Little Boy Blue Shirt

I hate seeing little boys trussed up in miniature city shirts and bow ties for formal wear, so when I found a 1920s child's silk tussah shirt with short sleeves and charming smocked detail I decided to reinterpret it as a modern special-occasion top, to pair with velvet knickerbockers for a pageboy or smart long trousers for a party guest. The style would work for a little girl, too – think how delightful boy and girl twins would look in contrasting colours – and could be fashioned in cotton lawn for more everyday occasions.

FINISHED SIZE

36 cm/14 in to hem; chest 84 cm/33 in (three-year-old). See page 130 for patterns for up to five-year-old sizes.

LEVEL

Intermediate. Skills required: machine-seam, setting in a sleeve, creating a collar placket, buttonholing.

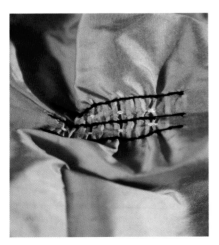

MATERIALS

2 m/2 yd light blue silk dupion
Basting thread
Sewing thread in the colour of the fabric
Dark navy and white thread in a deeper
    tone of the fabric colour
3 smart buttons

HOW TO CHEAT

Hate making buttonholes? You could use invisible press studs to close the placket, sewing the buttons on top. Don't feel bad about skimping the job: little ones can find small buttons problematic, so they won't see this kind of fastening as second-best.

Create a contrast Why not make up the design in white cotton with a pale blue collar and embroidery, inspired by this 1930s illustration.

METHOD

1 Photocopy and enlarge the pattern pieces (see page 130).

2 Position the pattern pieces on the silk fabric in the grain direction marked and cut out, including the 1.5 cm/⅜ in seam allowance.

3 Mark the dots to gather for the smocked areas with tailor's chalk.

4 Working across the marked dots, gather the four areas to be smocked (front and back of the shirt) with basting thread.

5 Using the blue and the white embroidery thread embroider the smocked areas in outline stitch and simple smocking stitch (see page 122), then remove the basting thread.

6 With right sides together, stitch the side seams of the shirt. Press.

7 At the top of the shirt front, on both sides of the neckline, position the top and the underside shoulder pieces, sandwiching the raw edge of the shirt front between them.

8 Working on the right side of the fabric, top-stitch. Press. Then repeat with the back seam.

9 Fold under the hem allowance on the sleeves; top-stitch to finish.

10 With right sides together, baste both sleeves in position and stitch. Press.

11 Using your buttonhole machine foot, make three buttonholes at the marked positions on the wider placket piece. Top-stitch both sides of the placket in place, making sure that you enclose the raw edges of the shirt front.

12 Right sides together, seam the collar underside and top together along the two short and one long side, leaving the second long side open.

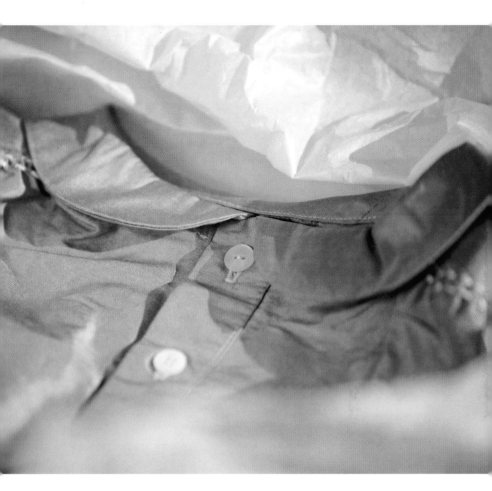

13 With right sides together, seam the outside edge of the collar to the neckline of the shirt, matching notches. Press.

14 Fold under the seam allowance on the inside edge of the collar and press. Slip-stitch or top-stitch the inside edge of the collar to the inside of the neckline. Press.

15 Fold under the hem allowance on the shirt body; top-stitch to finish.

Peter Pan collar This style of collar was named after the forever-young hero of the popular children's book by J.M. Barrie.

Rosy Purse

Sew pretty! This dear little purse, with its forty-four petals folded from soft pink cotton sateen ribbon, is just the thing for your budding party girl. The 1930s handbag design that inspired the Rosy Purse was intended to serve as an accessory for a young bridesmaid – somewhere for her to keep her lace handkerchief, along with some rose petals to strew before the bride.

FINISHED SIZE
One-size.

LEVEL
Easy. Skills required: Machine-seaming; hand-stitching; stab-stitch.

MATERIALS
0.5 m/$\frac{1}{2}$ yd pale-pink cotton fabric

0.5 m/$\frac{1}{2}$ yd white cotton, for lining

3 m /3$\frac{1}{4}$ yd pale pink 4 cm-/1$\frac{1}{2}$ in-wide cotton sateen ribbon

1 m/1 yd pale-pink 1 cm-/$\frac{3}{8}$ in-wide cotton sateen ribbon

Purchased ribbon rosebud

25 cm/10 in canvas

HOW TO CHEAT
You could skip Steps 1 through 4, and buy a little circular fabric bag. Then you just start from Step 5 to make the rose.

METHOD

1 Cut out four circles 18 cm/7 in in diameter from the pale pink cotton, and four from the white lining cotton.

2 With right sides together, take two pink cotton circles and place a cotton lining circle above and below them.

3 Stitch all four circles together, leaving a small opening to turn right (pink) sides out. Turn, then stitch the remaining seam invisibly. Join the other two pink cotton circles and two white interlinings in the same way. Press.

Blooming bridesmaid This charming 1930s design for a young bridesmaid inspired today's pretty party bag.

4 Pin both circles right sides together, stitching at the extreme edge around three-quarters of the circle. Turn and press.

5 Now begin making the petals with the ribbon. Cut the ribbon into 6 cm /2$\frac{1}{4}$ in lengths. At one end of a length, fold under two triangles, right sides facing. Stitch together about 6 mm/$\frac{1}{4}$ in from the top raw edge. Turn right sides out, and with scissor points shape into a neat mitre. Turn up the lower raw edge 6 mm/$\frac{1}{4}$ in and gather it. Pull up the gathers and fasten securely.

6 Make 13 more petals and stitch them around the outer edge of the purse, points facing to the outside of the circle.

7 Cut out a foundation circle 16.5 cm/6$\frac{1}{4}$ in in diameter from canvas. Now make four further petals, using the method in Step 5. Stitch one to a circular foundation canvas, then one below it, pointing downwards, one to the left and another to the right, all with the gathered edges facing to the centre of the circle.

8 Make another four petals, and stitch them into the canvas, behind and in between the first four.

9 Next make eight petals. Stitch behind and in between the first two lots of four.

10 Last round, make 12 petals. Stitch behind and in between the previous row of petals. Trim away any surplus canvas and stitch the canvas circle in the centre of the purse.

11 Sew the ribbon rosebud in the centre of the petals. To make a strap for your rosy purse, cut ribbon to your desired length and neatly stitch to the inside.

Soft centre A delicate ribbon rosebud replaces the wire and wax stamens that were used in the vintage design.

Wrappings

Complement your efforts to make a vintage-themed gift with appropriate wrappings. Look for vintage or vintage-style gift boxes, paper, ribbon and other trimmings. Staples like tissue paper and white woven ribbon, or even brown paper and string, will lend a traditional air.

GIFT-WRAP MEMORIES

If you are lucky, you may be able to find a vintage gift wrap like the 1940s stork paper, right. Make sure that the recipient is aware that it's a collectable paper. Wrap it around a box, covering the lid and base separately, so that once she has opened the box and enjoyed the gift inside she will re-use it (it would make a great photo storage box).

RIBBON PRESENT FROM THE PAST

Don't just think about pressing your vintage ribbon haul into use in your sewing projects. Why not use one to finish off your wrapped gift so that it becomes part of the present? For example, the tissue-paper-covered box (left) might contain a pretty dress that would be complemented by using the crisp silk gingham vintage ribbon as a hair bow or a sash for the dress.

VINTAGE WALLPAPER

Its rare to find enough vintage wallpaper to cover even one wall of a nursery, so if your discovery is just a scrap or part-roll, why not consider using it to wrap a gift? It could be kept afterwards and framed or used for a scrapbooking project. Another idea is to cut out motifs and découpage them on to a painted chest of drawers for your child's bedroom.

Baby's Trunk

Baby can show off a confident crawl in the sturdiest **down-home overalls**, make grandma melt in the dearest little **rick-rack yoke dress**, be the belle of the beach in the cutest **spot sunbonnet**, wow playdate pals with the simplest **marigold sunsuit**, and at the end of the day you can sing her to sleep with the **sweetest lullaby**.

Down-Home Overalls

Dungarees are the cutest coveralls for a crawling baby. The naïve print fabric on this vintage American pair has an unusual origin: food packaging. In the early twentieth century frugal farmers' wives made utilitarian garments and quilts out of the cotton feed sacks that dry goods were packed in. Canny suppliers soon cottoned on and started producing pretty pattern-printed sacks to boost sales.

FINISHED SIZE
To fit a one-, two- or three-year-old.

LEVEL
Intermediate. Skills required: simple machine-seam; sewing around a curve; machine-buttonhole (follow the instructions for your machine); sewing on a button.

MATERIALS
1 m/1 yd printed cotton
Remnant toning plain cotton for edgings
Matching thread
2 buttons

HOW TO CHEAT
There are several ways you can break the rules when choosing fabric. Can't find feed-sack material? Then why not make up the overalls in a print that has an edible connection, such as a delicious strawberry print. If you want an authentic feedsack pattern, there are companies producing reproductions.

Button alert On vintage garments make sure buttons are well fixed, as loose ones could be a choking hazard.

METHOD

1 Photocopy and enlarge the pattern pieces (see page 132). Pin the pattern pieces to the fabric, following the direction of the grain, and cut out.

2 Right sides together, stitch the leg seams. With right sides together, stitch the contrast band around the bottom of the leg. Fold the band over in half and slip-stitch in place on the reverse of the fabric. Press.

3 Join the two halves, right sides together, by sewing the central seam. Press.

4 With right sides together, machine-stitch the sides to the marked notch. Turn under the seam allowance on the open areas, slip-stitch in place.

5 With right sides together, attach the waistband to the trouser section. Fold in half, and slip-stitch on the reverse. Press.

6 Turn under the seam allowance on the top and side edges of the bib section and top-stitch. Press.

7 With right sides together, sew the bottom edge of the bib to the trouser section. Press.

8 Sew buttons firmly to either side of the top front edge of the bib. Make sure all buttons are very securely sewn on, so that the baby cannot chew them off and choke on them.

9 Fold the two strap pieces in half, right sides together; press. Seam, then turn right side out.

10 Make the buttonholes in one end of each strap; attach the other end to the back of the trouser section.

Feedsack style Sturdy rompers hand-stitched from printed fabric packaging in Depression-era America.

Rick-Rack Yoke Dress

I adore rick-rack, so this chic and easy dress was the perfect opportunity to garner in bolts of this beautiful trim. I prefer quality pure-cotton versions – you need to take more care when sewing, but the overall effect is crisper and more authentically vintage. I picked out three shades of pink to tone with some of the coloured spots on the white cotton piqué fabric I'd selected. If the fabric had been plain I would have chosen a trio of colours – patriotic red, white and navy on white linen or crayon hues of yellow, green and blue on red cotton, for example.

FINISHED SIZE

Chest 44 cm/17 in: length 50 cm/20 in (two-year-old size). See page 133 for patterns up to four-year-old sizes.

LEVEL

Easy. Skills required: Machine-seam; attaching trim.

MATERIALS

1.25 m/1³/₄ yd rick-rack in pale pink
1.25 m/1³/₄ yd rick-rack in medium pink
1.25 m/1³/₄ yd rick-rack in deep pink
1 m/1 yd of embroidered cotton piqué
Matching thread
2 press studs

HOW TO CHEAT

If you have a sewing machine with a special trimming attachment you can assemble the yoke much faster by top-stitching the rick-rack in place. Run the stitching down the middle of each rick-rack row and use invisible thread to lessen the impact of the line.

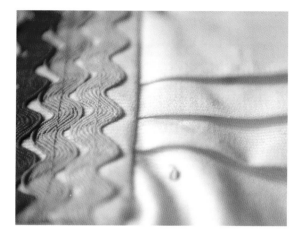

Colour and texture Look for inventive combinations. Here jumbo rickrack in 3 shades of pink wriggles across a cotton piqué with embroidered dots.

METHOD

1 Photocopy and enlarge the pattern pieces (see page 133). Following the direction of the grain, pin the pattern pieces to the fabric and cut out.

2 Pin rick-rack to the right sides of front yoke and shoulder-strap sections, spacing evenly and arranging with the darkest hue at the outer edge of each strap. Hand-stitch in place using a hidden prick-stitch.

3 With right sides together, seam the shoulder-strap fronts to their linings, leaving the bottom edge of the straps open. Turn right sides out and press.

4 Sandwich one end of each shoulder-strap between the yoke front and its lining, matching notches. With right sides of the yoke pieces together, seam the yoke front to its lining on top and side seams, leaving the bottom edge of the yoke open.

5 Matching the notches on the pattern pieces, make three box pleats in the front and the back of the skirt pieces and baste in place. Press pleats lightly.

6 Apply the side facings to the side edges of the back and front skirt pieces, right sides together. Seam; clip curves; press lightly; turn.

7 Pin the right side of the front and back skirt pieces to the yoke pieces, keeping the yoke lining free. Seam and press. Slip-stitch the yoke linings to the wrong sides of the skirt pieces.

8 Stitch two sets of press studs at the armhole edges on both sides.

9 Turn up the hem allowance to your required length (if you want the dress to serve for two summers, allow extra for growth). Press. Slip-stitch.

Two summers' length The dress can be made ankle or knee-length, to your preference. In the past, summer dresses were often made with room to grow.

Spot Sunbonnet

A charming trio of 1940s print sunbonnets inspired me to devise a new version without the ties and with a longer panel at the back to give more sun protection. So little fabric is required for this design that you can use up squirreled remnants from your own dressmaking. And if you are not a hoarder, it is a good excuse to indulge in an expensive fabric or a mad pattern. I chose an inexpensive design with giant spots the size of coins for the bonnet shown here. If you are making a summer dress for your little girl, why not buy enough fabric to make a matching bonnet that will provide some vital sun protection.

FINISHED SIZE
To fit a two- to three-year-old toddler.

LEVEL
Easy. Skills required: machine-seam; top-stitch.

MATERIALS
45 cm/^{1}/$_2$ yd printed cotton fabric
22 cm/^{1}/$_4$ yd plain cotton fabric
Medium-weight interfacing for brim
Matching thread

Polka dotty Crisp glazed cotton spotted with coin-sized polka dots brings out sunny smiles and shields sensitive skin. For greater protection, line the bonnet with sunproof fabric.

METHOD

1 Photocopy and enlarge the pattern pieces for the brim (see page 131). Cut a rectangle 55 cm/21$\frac{1}{2}$ in long and 22 cm/8$\frac{1}{2}$ in wide for the main part of the hat and a rectangle 35 cm/13 in long and 16 cm/6$\frac{1}{2}$ in wide for the neck section. Cut out. Cut a brim piece from interfacing and a second main section for the lining.

2 Right sides together, interfacing on top, seam brim pieces around 1 long and 2 short sides. Trim seam. Turn; press.

3 Top-stitch the right side of brim with four rows of stitching, starting inside the long edge. Fold the bonnet in half, right sides together, and stitch the back seam. Repeat with bonnet lining. Trim seams.

4 With right sides together, pin brim around face edge. Pin right side of bonnet lining over the brim, sandwiching brim between bonnet and lining. Seam; press.

5 Machine-hem a double 6 mm ($\frac{1}{4}$ in) hem at the bottom and side edges of the neck section. Make tucks at the bonnet neck. Pin lower edge of bonnet to neck section, right sides together, pleating to fit. Stitch. Trim seam. Press. Finish by slip-stitching a bias strip over the seam.

Marigold Sunsuit

Sunny mercerized cotton knits up into a delightful all-in-one playsuit for the beach or garden sandpit. I adapted the simple stocking-stitch design, doubling up the front bib at the back of the suit, so that your sandcastle-making toddler has some extra coverage (you'll still need to cover your child in a good-quality, high-factor sun cream, though). Make sure that your tension is correct; tightly woven or knitted fabrics give better sun protection.

FINISHED SIZE
To fit a two- to three-year-old toddler.

LEVEL
Easy. Skills required: Stocking-stitch; shaping.

MATERIALS
6 x 50g $^1/_4$ oz Rowan Cotton Glace, shade 825 Marigold Yellow
Size 3.25 mm knitting needles
Sewing needle
Small amount yellow cotton lining fabric

GAUGE/TENSION
23 stitches and 32 rows to 10 cm/4 in over stocking stitch.

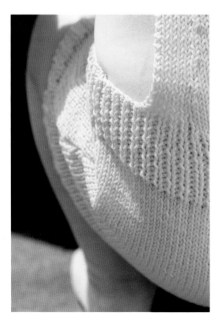

METHOD

Front (worked from the crotch upwards)

Cast on 15 sts.

Work in stocking stitch, casting on 2 sts at the end of each row until there are 87 sts.

Dec 1 st at both ends of every 6th row until 71 sts remain.

Work straight in stocking stitch until the piece measures 23 cm/9 in from the cast-on edge (measure down the middle of the piece).

Work tightly in K1, P1 rib for 3.5 cm/ 1¹⁄₂ in.

Cast off 10 sts at the beginning of the next 2 rows.

Frilled to bits Back in the 1950s mother and daughter were thrilled to have matching cotton swimsuits; perhaps not the done thing today.

Now start working the Bib.

1st row With right side facing, K1, P1 5 times; slip 1; K1; psso; K to the last 12 sts; K2 tog; P1, K1 5 times.

2nd row P1, K1 5 times; P to the last 10 sts; K1, P1 5 times.

3rd row K1, P1 5 times; K to the last 10 sts; P1, K1 5 times.

Repeat 2nd and 3rd rows alternately, decreasing (as on 1st row) every 6th row until 39 sts remain.

Work in K1, P1 rib for 2 cm/³⁄₄ in.

Next row With right side facing, K1, P1 5 times; cast off next 19 sts, working in rib. Work the next 10 sts in K1, P1 rib for 28 cm/11 in to form one strap.

Work the first 10 sts in the same manner to form the other strap.

Back

Work as for Front.

Leg Bands

Sew crotch seam.

With right side facing, pick up 88 sts along leg opening.

Work in K1, P1 rib for 2 cm/³⁄₄ in.

Cast off loosely in rib.

To finish:

Sew side seams.

Line straps with fabric to prevent stretching.

Sew strap ends to the back bib.

Press lightly.

Bedtime Lullabies and Tales

Not everything you create for your child requires a needle and thread: you can tailor them a story or weave an old melody into their dreams, introducing a handmade spirit into their bedtime routine. Use tales and songs handed down to you and carry on family traditions, or create new ones by looking for stories and rhymes that touch your heart.

PRECIOUS LULLABIES

Traditional lullabies have been tried and tested by generations, with reason. Research shows that singing to your child helps them sleep and encourages bonding between the two of you. As the child grows, repeating the words of their favourite bedtime song helps speech and language development. Additionally, exposure to music is said to help build neural pathways in the growing infant, improving their potential for learning.

STORYTIME

As your baby becomes a toddler, a bedtime story will often take the place of a lullaby. Just ten minutes at the end of the day will provide a special space for a parent with their child and bring literacy benefits when the child later starts school.

Little Tom Tucker,
He sang for his supper.
What did he sing for?
Why, white bread and butter.
How can I cut it without a knife?
How can I marry without a wife?

35

Little Tommy Tucker Heading for a talent show in an adorable suit.

HUSH A BYE BABY

It is said that a pilgrim father wrote this rhyme after observing Native American babies hung in the branches of trees:

Hush-a-bye Baby on the tree top
When the wind blows the cradle will rock
When the wind ceases the cradle will fall
Down will come cradle and baby and all.

Toddler's Closet

Knit a warm wool **striped sweater** for a cuddly winter child and make every day special for your little girl with a crisp linen **lazy daisy pinafore** scattered with hand-embroidered lazy daisies. Run up a marshmallow-soft **ruffle dress** and **bloomers** and watch her party in your sugar-pink confection, or stitch a classic **sailor top** in marine blue poplin for a smart summer boy.

striped sweater

A charming 1920s sweater designed to be worked in two shades: pilot blue and natural grey. The photograph on the original pattern leaflet was in black and white, so I decided to see how the colours suggested would look.

I chose marine blue as the major colour, for the larger stripes and the ribbed bottom band, collar and cuffs. I varied the design just a little by picking two different shades of grey for the finer stripes and alternating them.

SIZE
To fit a four-year-old.
Chest measurement: 54 cm/21¼ in.

LEVEL
Easy. Skills required: Garter-stitch; K1, P1 rib; increasing and decreasing; buttonhole.

MATERIALS
400 g/14 oz Rowan Pure Wool DK,
   shade 008 Marine
100 g/3½ oz Rowan in Pure Wool DK,
   shade 002 Shale
100 g/3½ oz Rowan in Pure Wool DK,
   shade 003 Anthracite
3 mm needles
Size 3.75 mm needles
2 buttons

HOW TO CHEAT
If you don't want to tackle knitting a button loop, or your child finds them difficult when dressing, then use invisible press studs instead.

GAUGE/TENSION
10 stitches and 10 rows to 4 cm/1½ in over garter stitch.

METHOD
Back

Using 3 mm needles and Marine Blue yarn, cast on 80 sts.

1st row Working into back of sts, *K1, P1. Repeat from * to end.

2nd row *K1, P1. Repeat from * to end.

Repeat the 2nd row until work measures 5 cm/2¹/₂ ins.

Next row K.

Change to 3.75 mm needles and work in garter stitch (every row knitted), working in stripes as follows:

** Using blue yarn K 8 rows. Break off yarn.

Join light grey yarn, K 6 rows Break off yarn.

Rejoin blue yarn, K 12 rows. Do not break off yarn.

Short and sweet Short trousers were the order of the day for little boys. The pattern for the 1930s design I based this sweater on came with matching knitted shorts.

Join dark grey yarn, K 2 rows. Break off yarn.**

Repeat from ** to ** twice more.

Shape armholes as follows:

1st row Using blue yarn, cast off 4 sts, K to end.

2nd row Cast off 4 sts, K to end.

3rd row K2 tog, K to last 2 sts, K2 tog.

4th row As 3rd row (60 sts remain).

Keeping continuity of stripes, work in garter stitch until you have worked five narrow dark-grey stripes from commencement, finishing after a narrow dark grey stripe. Break off yarn.

Shape shoulders as follows:

1st row Using blue yarn, K to last 6 sts; turn.

2nd row K to last 6 sts; turn.

3rd and 4th rows K to last 12 sts; turn.

5th and 6th rows K to last 18 sts; turn.

7th row K to end.

Cast off.

Front

Work exactly as instructions for Back, as far as completion of armhole shaping. 60 sts remain.

Using blue yarn, K 4 rows. Break off yarn. Join on light grey yarn and K 6 rows. Break off yarn.

Divide for front opening as follows:

Next row Join on blue yarn and K 30 sts. Slip remaining 30 sts onto a yarn holder; turn.

Working on first set of sts for left half of front; K 11 rows in blue, 2 rows in dark grey; 8 rows in blue and 3 rows in light grey, finishing at front edge.

Shape Neck as follows:

1st row Still using light grey yarn, cast off 6 sts; K to end.

2nd row K.

3rd row K2 tog; K to end. Break off yarn. Join on blue yarn and repeat 2nd and 3rd row 5 times more (18 sts remain).

Join dark grey yarn, K2 rows. Break off yarn.

Shape Shoulder as follows:

1st row Using blue yarn, K.

2nd row K to last 6 sts; turn.

3rd row K to neck.

4th row K to last 12 sts; turn.

5th row K to neck.

Cast off knitwise.

Slip remaining 30 sts from holder onto a 3.75 mm needle, point to centre. Rejoin blue yarn and proceed for right half.

Keeping order of stripes correct, K 24 rows, finishing at front edge.

Shape Neck as follows:

1st row Using pale grey yarn, cast off 6 sts; K to end.

2nd row K.

3rd row K2 tog; K to end.

4th row K. Break off yarn.

5th row Joining blue yarn, K2 tog; K to end.

6th row K.

7th row K2 tog; K to end.

8th row K.

Repeat 7th and 8th row 3 times more (18 sts remain).

Using blue yarn, K2 rows.

Joining pale grey yarn, K2 rows, finishing at neck edge. Break off yarn.

Shape Shoulder as follows:

1st row Using blue yarn, K to last 6 sts; turn.

2nd row K to neck.

3rd row K to last 12 sts; turn.

4th row K to neck.

Cast off purlwise.

Sleeve

Using 3 mm needles and blue yarn, cast on 42 sts.

1st row Working into back of sts, *K1, P1. Repeat from * to end.

2nd row *K1, P1. Repeat from * to end.

Repeat 2nd row 18 times more.

21st row *K5, K2 tog. Repeat from * to end (36 sts remain).

Change to 3.75 mm needles and continue in garter st, following same order of stripes as on Back, increasing by working into front and back of first st and last st but one on 9th row, and every 6th row following, until there are 64 sts on needle. Keeping order of sts correct, continue without further shaping, until work measures 23 cm/9 in from commencement.

Shape Top as follows:

Keeping stripes correct, cast off 4 sts at beg of each of next 2 rows.

Decrease 1 st at both ends of every following row, until 16 sts remain.

Cast off.

Work a second sleeve.

Collar

Using No 11 needles and blue yarn, cast on 86 sts.

1st row Working into back of sts, *K1, P1. Repeat from * to end.

2nd row *K1, P1. Repeat from * to end.

Repeat 2nd row twice more.

Keeping continuity of rib, increase 1 st at both ends of next row, and every alternate row following, until there are 94 sts left.

Continue in rib, without further shaping, for 10 rows.

Cast off in rib.

To make up:

Carefully weave in ends of yarn.

Omitting ribbing, press work on wrong side, using a hot iron and damp cloth.

Join Shoulders of Back and Front together.

Stitch sleeves into position.

Stitch side and sleeve seams.

Place cast-on edge of collar to neck edge and, commencing and finishing 6 mm/¼ in from Front opening, stitch collar around neck.

Make two button loops on left side of Front by twisting two strands of yarn together. Attach two buttons on Right side of Front to correspond.

Best dressed Like teddy's dickey bow, the neckline of this striped sweater reveals its traditional roots.

Lazy Daisy Pinafore

A 1920s schoolroom pinafore, which would have been worn over a print dress, is just the thing to top today's pink cotton tee and leggings. The easy embroidery design means that most likely the pinny was stitched with love by big sister in her sewing lesson. Even if you are a novice you'll be able to run up my modern version in no time if you follow the instructions here. And if you want to skip class, read How to Cheat below to discover a sneaky short cut.

SIZE
Fits a four-year-old child.

LEVEL
Easy. Skills required: Simple machine-hemming; buttonhole-stitch; blanket-stitch, lazy daisy stitch, whipped running-stitch and French knots (see page 124).

MATERIALS
1.4 m-/1½ yd-wide white linen fabric

White cotton sewing thread

2 skeins black embroidery thread

Small amount of pink and yellow embroidery thread

90 cm/1 yd 2.5-cm/1-in wide pink gingham ribbon (optional if you don't want to make piping)

2 white buttons

Embroidery needle

HOW TO CHEAT
Find an old embroidered tablecloth from a charity shop or some other second-hand source and use two of the corner motifs for the pockets, and one for the neckline decoration. You can turn the fourth motif into a little dolly bag for your child to put her hanky in. If your cloth has plenty of white ground you may be able to cut the body of the pinafore from it, too.

Open here The back of this 1920s pinny has a simple v-shaped opening, outlined confidently in black running stitch.

METHOD

1 Photocopy and enlarge the pattern pieces (see page 135). Following the marked direction of the grain, pin the pattern pieces to the fabric and cut out.

2 With right sides together, stitch the shoulder seams. Press.

3 Turn under the hem allowance on the neckline. Press. Pin around the gingham piping or ribbon so that 1 cm/$^1/_3$ in is on show. Top-stitch in place. Press.

4 Turn under the hem allowance all around the sides and bottom of the pinafore. Machine-stitch. Press.

5 Work a line of whipped running stitch in black embroidery thread along the sides

and hem of the pinafore, about 5 cm/2 in in from the edge.

6 In black embroidery thread, work two lines of whipped running-stitch around the neckline, 3 cm/1$^1/_2$ in from the edge.

7 Next, work on the decorative embroidery panel. Measure and mark the central point for the bottom of the longest line of running-stitch. Mark the position of the circle and central French knots that make up the middle of the daisies. Using primrose-yellow embroidery thread, work the French knots, then switch to pink thread for the daisy petals and finally green thread for their leaves. Now return to the black thread and work the vertical whipped running-stitch lines, finishing each with a small French knot.

8 To make a pocket, turn under the hem allowance on the top edge. Press. Pin around the gingham piping or ribbon so that 1 cm/$^1/_3$ in is on show. Top-stitch in place. Press. Measure and mark the central point and the position for the daisies on the fabric, following the photograph as a guide. Work the design in whipped running-stitch, lazy daisy stitch and French knots. Press. Make a second pocket in the same way.

9 Turn under the seam allowance on the remaining three sides of the pocket and stitch the pockets in place on the front of the pinafore.

10 On the front of the pinafore, 3 cm/1½ in from the top of the straight edge, make two buttonholes by hand, using black embroidery thread and buttonhole stitch. Sew the two buttons onto the right side of the back of the pinafore to line up with the buttonholes on the pinny front.

Vintage cover-up Before the days of washing machines mothers often shielded their little girl's best dresses with a pretty pinny to keep them pristine so they could be handed down to younger sisters.

Ruffle Dress

A mini-flapper shift dress is simple in style, yet far from plain, with its tiers of applied ruffles on the skirt. The 1920s original that inspired me was in buttercup-yellow silk crepe, with three pale-pink ribbon rosebuds decorating the peaks of the top row of ruffles. I selected cotton voile, called dotted Swiss, for my version, in pale pink with white dots. As I planned to make matching ruffled bloomers in fine pale-pink cotton poplin (see page 90), the fabric's semi-sheer quality was an advantage. And as the ribbon rosebuds I found were smaller than the original ones, I used five.

SIZE

Chest: 88 cm/34 in (four-year-old). See page 136 for patterns for other sizes.

LEVEL

Easy. Skills required: Machine-seam; ruffle edging technique.

MATERIALS

1 1/2 m/1 1/2 yd dotted Swiss cotton in pale pink
5 ribbon rosebuds
Matching thread
2 press studs

HOW TO CHEAT

Instead of finishing the edges of your ruffles by machine, take the easier, modern approach and fray them. Before starting on your cut ruffles, pull a few threads on a sample piece of fabric as a test. Only pull two or three threads from each side, or before you know it your ruffle will be reduced to a pile of threads.

Flapper fashion The dotted Swiss cotton voile ruffle dress opposite was based on this egg-yolk yellow 1920s original in floaty silk crepe de chine. The front of the vintage dress is also shown on page 117.

3 Stitch the centre back piece (godet) to one side seam using a French seam.

4 Attach the ruffles to the front of the dress, stitching down the centre of the ruffle. Follow the picture on page 117 for placement. Position the ribbon roses and sew them in place.

5 Stitch the remaining centre back seam with a French seam. With right sides together, stitch the shoulder seams.

6 Make a 10 cm-/4 in-long placket (see page 123) at the top of the centre-back piece. Sew on press studs to close.

7 Turn under the hem allowance on the armholes, then, working on the right side of the dress, baste on the ruffles and top-stitch in place, running the stitch down the centre of the ruffle.

8 Run a gathering thread along front and back neck edges. Finish with a bias piece made from your fabric.

METHOD

1 Photocopy and enlarge the pattern pieces on page 136. Following the marked direction of the grain, pin the pattern pieces to the fabric and cut out. For the ruffles: cut with grain running across the width of the fabric.

2 Finish both edges of each ruffle strip using the zigzag foot or follow the 'cheat's option' of fraying the edges (see page 87).

Sheer delight If you use a sheer fabric like our dotted voile, you'll need a petticoat or a plain cotton underdress.

Ruffle Bloomers

Generously gathered and frilled panties, or bloomers, are a charming vintage look and prettily conceal nappies on younger toddlers. A pale-pink cotton poplin pair tone perfectly with the Ruffle Dress on page 86 to make just the thing to wear to a party. You could make another pair in white poplin, replacing the ruffles with rick-rack, to make a partner to go with the charming Rick-Rack Yoke Dress on page 60.

SIZE
See page 131 for patterns for three- to five-year-old sizes.

LEVEL
Easy. Skills required: Machine-seam; Ruffle edging technique.

MATERIALS
50 cm/½ yd pale-pink cotton poplin
10 cm/¼ yd contrasting fabric for the
    ruffle (I have chosen the Dotted Swiss
    used for the Ruffle Dress, see page 86)
Matching thread
1 m/1 yd of 12 mm-/½ in-wide sateen
ribbon

Just frilled Light-as-a-feather dotted Swiss cotton voile frills are interspersed with creamy pink cotton sateen.

METHOD

1 Photocopy and enlarge the pattern on page 131. Pin the pattern to the fabric and cut out.

2 Make the ruffles: cut out 6 30 cm-/12 in-long and 2.5 cm-/1 in-wide strips.

3 Finish both edges of each ruffle strip using the zigzag foot on your machine.

4 Attach the ruffles to the front and back of the bloomers, following the photograph for positioning. Stitch the ribbon casing in position following the marked line on the pattern (see page 131).

5 With right sides together, stitch the inner leg seams. Press.

6 With right sides together, stitch the crotch seam. Press.

7 Thread through the leg elastic, gather and secure. Finish the openings for the elastic with a few stitches.

8 With right sides together, turn under the waistband hem allowance and stitch in place, leaving the inside ends open to take the elastic. Press.

9 Thread through elastic, gather and secure. Finish opening with slip-stitches.

Sugar-pink leggings Bloomers are the vintage equivalent of today's leggings and a delightfully fancy modesty solution for a too-short dress.

Sailor Top

Sailor outfits for children have been popular since the nineteenth century, when European royals first set the trend. Originally worn by boys with short or long trousers, by the early twentieth century sailor tops paired with skirts were fashionable for girls, too. The sailor suit is now a classic, generally for pageboy or first-communion wear. This cotton poplin version was adapted from a French one from around 1910. The original was in winter-wear serge.

SIZE
Chest 56 cm/22 in (to fit a three-year-old). See page 134 for patterns up to five-year-old sizes.

LEVEL
Intermediate. Skills required: machine-seam; attaching collar; adding braid.

MATERIALS
1.25 m/1³/₄ yd cotton poplin in chosen colour
1.25 m/1³/₄ yd of wide 2.5 cm/1 in petersham for hems
1 m/1 yd of narrow 1 cm-/¹/₂ in-wide cotton petersham to trim collar
Matching thread

HOW TO CHEAT
If you buy folded petersham, you'll only need one seam to finish the edges. Pin the petersham over the raw hem edges. Top-stitch in place to finish.

METHOD

1 Photocopy and enlarge the pattern pieces on page 134. Pin the pattern pieces to the fabric and cut out.

2 With right sides together, stitch the shoulder seams. Press.

3 Press the seam allowance on the poplin on all hems to the right side. Pin the petersham to cover the raw edge, matching the fold on the seam allowance with the finished edge on the petersham. Top-stitch top and bottom of petersham in place. Press.

4 With right sides together, stitch the side seams. Press.

5 Trim the upper collar piece with petersham. Position the petersham 2.5 cm/1 in from the outside edge of the collar. Start with the short edge and place the long edge on top.

6 Place the upper and underside of the collar pieces right sides together; seam around the three outer sides; clip corners if necessary to ensure crisp points. Turn the collar right side out. Press.

7 With right sides together, baste, then machine-stitch the collar underside to the neck edge.

8 Slip-stitch the collar upper side in place over the raw edges.

9 Fold the sleeve in half, right sides together, and machine-stitch the arm seam. Press. Repeat with the second sleeve.

10 With right sides together, pin the sleeve into the armhole, easing around the curve. Baste, clip curves, then stitch the sleeve into the armhole. Repeat with the second sleeve. Press.

Beach belles Like the sunsuit and smocks in this vintage illustration, the sailor top is a traditional choice for sunny days at the seaside – and with its long sleeves it provides some contemporary sun protection.

Hang it all Sailor suits were traditionally made in white poplin for summer and navy serge for winter. Often, the collar would be in a contrast fabric as well as the trim. The collar and tie would be removable for cleaning. In this version the main body is in 100 percent cotton, as is the petersham ribbon, so you can pop the whole thing in the washing machine.

Will You Come to my Party?

In the 1930s most kids' party costumes were created at home. Mum worked with whatever was to hand: dusters, coloured paper, and clothes from the cupboard. Instead of a shop-bought outfit, enjoy being old-time inventive.

THE POKE BONNET

No one would guess that this young lady wears a nightdress with a blue ribbon sash and one of mum's scarves as a shawl. The poke bonnet is a circle of stiff white paper tied on with more blue ribbon.

LITTLE FRENCH FISHERGIRL

Start with a simple plain blue dress and tie on a checked duster as an apron. Use either red and black crêpe paper or fabric remnants to make the bodice and waist sash. To make the bonnet frill, pleat stiff white paper and fix it to your little girl's head with hair clips. A white ribbon bow tied around her head will complete the effect.

FIVE FINGER EXERCISES

A black crêpe paper yoke and oblong crêpe paper strips top a simple white frock to create this charming costume for a junior piano player. Cut out the letter L from a sheet of red paper and paste it to the front of the yoke. Finally, photocopy a sheet of music onto stiff paper to make the hat.

THE SHIRLEY POPPY

Cut out four petals from white crêpe paper. To create the shaded effect, paint them with diluted red ink, applied with a brush. Cut out a little yoke and collar from green crêpe paper and staple on the petals. To make the hat, take a band of red crêpe paper and gather one end with a red hair elastic, spreading out the paper above the elastic to form a flat, round frill.

THE CIRCUS CLOWN

Your little boy's sleepsuit is the basis of this fun outfit; if you don't own a striped suit, any plain bright colour will work just as well. Cut the cap and ruffles from white crêpe paper and the pom-poms from red and blue crêpe paper. String a cone of stiff red paper on elastic for the nose.

Nursery Life

There are plenty of pretty things you can make for your young child to use around the home. Mop up spills with the **rick-rack splat mat**, encourage a toddler to tidy away things to go in the wash with the **duck laundry bag** and celebrate a traditional Christmas with a cheerful knitted **candy cane Christmas stocking**. The chapter concludes with practical advice on vintage toy and crib safety.

Rick-Rack Splat Mat

Easy to launder and practical for travelling, this generous place mat for baby is made from two layers of absorbent terry trimmed in super-sized rick-rack braid. Once the meal is ended, wipe the table over with the mat and throw it in the washing machine so it is fresh for tomorrow. Or you might want to make two so that you have one to use and a spare in the wash.

FINISHED SIZE
48 cm x 33 cm/19 in x 13 in.

LEVEL
Extremely easy. Skills required: machine-seam.

MATERIALS
50 cm/^{2}/$_3$ yd terry towelling, 150 cm/60 in wide. Makes 3

1.5 m /1^1/$_2$ yd giant rick-rack braid per mat

Thread to match towelling

HOW TO CHEAT
It's so easy, so why would you? My short cut was to use two rows of giant rick-rack at both edges of the mat, rather than the three rows of regular rick-rack in the original version. You can get rick-rack in a range of sizes, from super-size to miniature. Just adjust the numbers of rows you stitch down to suit your time and inclination.

METHOD

1 Cut one rectangle of towelling 72 x 28 cm/20 x 14 in. Fold in half with right sides together. Allowing a 1.25 cm/^{1}/$_2$ in seam allowance, join the two oblongs, leaving 8 cm/3 in free. Clip corners.

2 Turn right side out. Machine-stitch around the mat, just inside the edge. Press.

3 Cut the length of rick-rack in two equal lengths. Turn under 6 mm/^{1}/$_4$ in at each end of each half. Hem. Press. Stitch a row of rick-rack down each short side of the cloth.

Duck Laundry Bag

Keeping the laundry in order can be a household nightmare. Clothes to be washed just seem to get scattered everywhere. Encourage your own little duckling to get into good habits by sewing them a fun laundry bag that can double as a toy – they all love ducks. I used cheerful checked gingham for the duck's body, as on page 107. You could substitute plain white cotton if you have some to hand – if it's a gift then it would suit any nursery colour scheme.

FINISHED SIZE
83 cm/ 32½ in.

LEVEL
Easy. Skills required: machine-seam.

MATERIALS
1 m/1 yd pink-checked
    gingham
Remnant white cotton
Remnant yellow cotton
Black embroidery silk
White cotton thread
Toy filling

Old Duck A 1920s illustration that inspired today's version.

METHOD

1 Photocopy and enlarge the pattern pieces on page 137.

2 Cut out the handle, neckband, and front and back of the bag from checked gingham. Cut out the front and back of the beak and the front and back of each foot from yellow cotton, and the front and back of the head from white cotton.

3 With right sides together and following the seam allowances, join the side and lower seams of the bag. Turn under the placket edging and machine-seam.

4 Press the neckband in half horizontally, then press under the seam allowances. Lay the neckband out flat, wrong side facing and pleat the front of the bag so that it covers half the neckband (both upwards and across). In the same way, pleat the back of the bag into the other half of the band. Turn right side out and top-stitch the bottom edge of the band in place. Fold the uncovered half of the band over the pleated top. Slip-stitch in place.

5 With right sides together join the short side of the left beak piece to the left side of the head and the short side of the right beak to the right side of the head.

Squeaky clean Hung on a hook or knob, this ingenious toy encourages your child to play the very tidy game of stuffing the duck's tummy with dirty linen.

6 With right sides together and following the seam allowances, and starting at the back of the neck, stitch right around the back of the head, under the beak and along the front neck.

7 Fill the head firmly. Slip-stitch it to the top opening of the bag inside the top of the neck band.

8 With right sides together, seam the two feet, turn right sides out and stuff lightly with filling.

9 Tuck in the 7.5 cm/3 in between the feet and press it flat.

10 Sew a foot each side of the base hem in the centre and 3.5 cm/1½ in away from the side seam.

In the swim Not just decorative, the bright yellow feet are carefully placed to help weight the bag when it's empty.

11 Fold the handle strip in half lengthways, wrong sides together. Turn it right side out.

12 Lay the two handle ends together side by side and stitch them to the back of the neck for 5 cm/2 in.

13 Embroider the duck's eyes in black silk, using stem-stitch. If your child is under the age of three, don't be tempted to sew on buttons or anything that can be removed by small hands as they are a swallow-hazard.

candy cane christmas Stocking

Today, Christmas stockings are the size of a giant's boot. Traditionally, they were skinnier and held just a few toys, an orange, and a handful of home-made sweets. Often parents hung up one of their own stockings, so I started with a 1920s plain bed sock pattern, but knitted it in the chunkiest of chunky yarns, to supersize it for twenty-first-century toys. And as I wanted to sweeten it up, I added a diagonal stripe in candy-cane red to the snowy-white base.

FINISHED SIZE
61 cm/24 in.

LEVEL
Intermediate. Skills required: 1 on 1 rib; eyelet holes, decreasing, increasing, following a colour chart.

MATERIALS
100 g/3½ oz Rowan Big Wool, shade 28 Bohemian (red)
200 g/7 oz Rowan Big Wool, shade 001 White Hot (white)
10 mm-long needles or a 10 mm circular needle
Crochet hook

HOW TO CHEAT
If you don't want to tackle the stripe, just knit it up in a plain yarn. I used a double-knit yarn for a smaller plain-rib stocking.

GAUGE/TENSION
10 stitches and 9 rows to 10 cm/4 in over stocking stitch.

METHOD

Work 2.5cm/1 in in K.1 P1 rib.

Make a row of ribbon holes:

1st row K1, *wf, K2 tog, repeat from * to the end of the row.

2nd row K each knitted stitch and K one strand of each double loop.

Continue again in rib until you have worked 7.5cm/3 in in rib.

Start working the candy-cane pattern, following the chart on page 129, until the work measures 46 cm/18 in from top of the cuff.

Switching to red yarn only, continuing in K1P1 rib, shape the toe as follows:

1st row K tog every 9th and 10th st.

2nd and every alternate row No shaping.

3rd row K tog every 8th and 9th stitch.

5th row K tog every 7th and 8th stitch.

Continue in this manner until only 15 sts remain. Run a thread through these sts and fasten off securely.

To finish

If you are concerned about presents snagging in the stranding inside, you could line the candy cane section of the stocking in a plain cream cotton fabric. Using the crochet hook and remaining yarn, join the back seam. Thread matching red ribbon through the holes at the top of the stocking and tie in a bow.

Stocking stuff What do you fill a stocking with? As the poem says: 'Something to eat, something to read, something to play with and something they need'.

Fasten with a ribbon Part of the fun of this stocking is untying the top – like a parcel. Don't use a tie like this for a child under 3 years, however, as it could be a choking hazard.

Safe in the Cradle

You'll want to create a completely safe environment for your baby or toddler, so it's vital to consider safety factors before you bring any vintage item into your nursery. For example, hand-knits may be so loose that little fingers can get caught, vintage clothes may include ribbons and buttons that could be a choking hazard and old cots may not reach today's safety standards.

CRIB WISDOM

Vintage nursery furniture, such as cribs and cots, will not be baby-proof by today's stringent standards, so if you want a vintage-style nursery it's probably wise to play safe and shop for a modern recreation. Serious, and even fatal, accidents have occurred in the past, where babies have tumbled from unsecured cot sides or trapped their heads between widely spaced bars (these must be between 2.5 and 6.5 cm/1 and 2½ in apart and there must be at least 51 cm/20 in between the top of the mattress and the top of the cot). So consign grandma's crib to the attic and shop for an up-to-date version.

CLOTHING CONCERNS

If you have inherited a wonderful vintage frock or found the sweetest pair of never-worn vintage satin slippers on sale, bear in mind that clothing safety standards today are much stricter than in former times and you may want to have the garment copied and adapted to take into account modern requirements.

TOY STORY

Many old toys, too, fail to meet our modern safety standards, for example toxic paints containing lead may have been used and moving parts may be loose or rusty. So any charming thrift-store finds or attic treasures are best kept just for display, safely out of baby's reach.

Your Practical Primer

Here you can learn all the **basic skills** you need to create the

20 easy-to-make projects, find practical advice on buying

and using both modern and **vintage tools** and **materials**, and

discover all the **pattern pieces** and information you will require

to make your chosen project.

Fabrics

A vintage-style design calls for an appropriately traditional fabric. Choose cotton in utility weaves such as drill or gingham for every day, or in smart finishes like piqué and dotted Swiss for special occasions.

PRINT OR PLAIN

Today, we use a broad palette for baby clothes, but what were the traditional colours for baby wear? Apart from pastel pink for girls or blue for boys, flower hues such as lavender and primrose yellow were perennially popular for babies. And white, for innocence, of course. For

Pretty in pastel Vintage floral print and plain lawn, seen here in traditional baby blue and pink

toddlers, colours and prints were often influenced by the fashions of the day. Certain prints – such as Liberty flower sprigs – are still in production. Other designs are being re-imagined or reproduced – from American feed sack patterns to cowboy imagery, from teddy bear motifs to polka dots. For information on where to find the fabrics used in this book, see page 144.

LAUNDERING ORIGINAL VINTAGE PIECES

Your made-new vintage design will be ready to wear once you have finished sewing. But what if you find an original vintage piece? If you want your child to wear it rather than using it as nursery decoration (a special but fragile dress hung from a hook on a painted wooden hanger can be prettier than a picture), then you are going to want it to be fresh-smelling and clean. If the item is delicate, hand-wash it in pure soap flakes. With sturdier items you can brave the washing machine if you are willing to risk shrinkage or dyes running.

Ruffle dress For a modern interpretation of this
little silk crepe-de-chine number, see page 86.

Tools

If you plan to make up sewn designs in this book in addition to the specific materials for the project, you will need a sewing machine, pins, needles, scissors, a tape measure, squared paper, and a gauge.

SEWING MACHINES

Unlike modern machines, vintage sewing machines are a gloriously decorative addition to your home, so if your requirements are simple you may want to own a piece of sewing history. Enamelled in shiny black, decorated with elaborate gold scrolls and set in solid wood bases (some even have their own table-like stands), they are inexpensive to buy and

Helpful hoops Stretch fabric for embroidery the traditional way, between wooden circles, tightening the brass screw to hold fabric taut.

there are specialists to be found who will repair and maintain them, and sell you accessories and spare parts. That said, today's machines are a dream to own – light to move about, simple to thread and capable of a dazzling array of stitches. Top-of-the-range models even connect to your computer so you can download your own machine-embroidery designs.

PINS AND NEEDLES

A hand-made vintage pincushion and needle case would keep your pins and needles prettily and safely. I adore those pins with beaded heads. They are easier to see in your fabric and they stand out when you have dropped them on the floor (no mother of crawlers wants sharp pins where small hands and feet are prowling). Make sure you have a good selection of needles, from sharps to a range of the embroidery sort.

SCISSORS

Invest in a pair of really good-quality scissors for cutting fabric and make sure that they never, ever get used for cutting paper. Small embroidery scissors are a

must, too. Stork-shaped ones (see page 33) are a delight, and can be found in silver or gold-plated finishes for a special gift, but regular types will do the job just as well. Fancy stork-handled scissors will be particularly fascinating to your kids, so take care to keep all your scissors well out of their reach.

PATTERN-DRAFTING TOOLS

You can scale up patterns on squared paper the traditional way, or use special software and your computer. There isn't space in this book to provide instructions for beginners, so if you haven't done it before, make sure that you look for information in your sewing manual or on the internet. To scale up patterns in this book enlarge them on a photocopier.

Old notions To make your own pin cushion, cut a circle of linen, embroider your design, stuff firmly with tightly packed polyester wadding, or the traditional emery filling, if you can find it, and gather tightly underneath.

EMBROIDERY HOOPS

If you are tackling any of the simple embroidery projects (the ABC Jeanius Blocks, the Lazy Daisy Pinafore or Skinny Monkey's features) then using a special embroidery hoop to stretch the fabric taut and hold it while you are working makes things a great deal easier. Hoops consist of two circles, usually made from wood. You place your fabric between the circles and tighten a screw to create tension. They come in lots of different sizes to suit your project.

Ribbons, Buttons and Bows

Adding the right trim is the fastest way to give anything a vintage air,

whether you choose everyday rick-rack or indulgent velvet ribbon,

pearly or plain linen buttons.

If you crave an authentic touch, and grandma's sewing box doesn't contain a whole rainbow of family heirlooms you can appropriate for the next generation, then hunt for vintage buttons, ribbon and other trimmings at flea markets and on internet auction sites. My recent hauls include a clutch of ready-embroidered ducks, all set to waddle across the front of a romper suit, reels of peppermint-striped grosgrain ribbon that will make the prettiest sashes or hair ribbons, and opaque glass buttons in the shape of

sweet little oranges that I am going to use to fasten a sunny smocked cotton jacket.

BUYING BUTTONS

You can still buy whole cards of unused vintage buttons, along with full sets carefully saved from clothes worn out decades ago. Can't find a whole set? Don't be afraid to mix and match – it's a modern twist that will really make the outfit original. Start by trying a harlequin set in shades of pink, from palest shell to deep carnation, and you will soon be experimenting with more daring mixes.

WORKING WITH RIBBON

Ribbon comes in a whole rainbow of qualities, widths and finishes. Silk ribbon can still be found at a price, but bear in

Vintage buttons Hunt for charming plastic buttons like these. Rinse them in an anti-bacterial liquid soap before use. It's best to avoid china, glass and real mother-of-pearl buttons for little ones, as they can snap, and baby could easily swallow a piece.

WORKING WITH TRIM

You may want to use strips of fabric, rather than ribbon, to create your project. For example, you could use gingham fabric, rather than gingham ribbon, for the neck and pocket edging of the pinafore on page 82. Though it will be a bit more work, the advantage is that you can use any fabric you like and this will give you a wider choice of effects if you can't find the ribbon you want. It will also give you the chance to use up scraps. To make a fabric trim, cut your strips on the bias and turn under along one side, pressing the fold with a hot iron.

mind that rayon arrived in the 1920s – it's so much easier on the pocket and is just as genuine. If you are going to sew the ribbon onto something, choose a single-faced type; if you are planning on a sash around the waist or ties at the back, look for the double-faced kind. Ribbon was widely used on vintage baby clothes, but today we are more aware about choking hazards and are less liberal with its use. If you do want to use it do make sure that all ribbon is stitched down firmly and avoid using sashes or ties for children who are under the age of three.

Ribbon-wrapped airer A wooden frame covered with satin ribbon or bias-cut strips was just the thing for airing baby clothes in a 1937 nursery.

Sewing Techniques

I have assumed that you either have basic sewing skills or, if you are a beginner, a good manual to help you. Most projects are simple, but there are a couple of specific techniques outlined in more detail here.

PRETTY LITTLE FRENCH SEAM

A chic yet tough finish that safely traps raw edges inside an enclosed seam, this finishing technique was often used on children's garments because it stands up to vigorous washing and reduces the risk of fraying. As it adds bulk, it works best on light fabrics.

1 With wrong sides together, sew just inside the seam line on the right side of the garment. At this stage, the raw edges of the seam will be seen on the outside of the garment. Trim these edges back to about $1/2$ cm/$1/8$ in.

2 Turn the garment to the wrong side and baste along the seam line. You should have trapped the raw edges inside the new seam, on the wrong side of the fabric. Machine-stitch. The French seam will be on the inside. Press.

MAKING A BIAS STRIP

Cut diagonally to the grain of the material. To do this, fold the material so that the weft thread is parallel to the selvedge. Then cut along, parallel to the fold. Repeat for more strips. Join strips together where necessary.

THE SIMPLEST SMOCKING

Elaborately smocked garments are a vintage delight. Learning this skill is part of a different book, but here are some basic instructions to help you work the very simple smocking used on the boy's shirt on page 44.

1 Use tailor's chalk or a dressmaking pencil to mark out evenly spaced dots as a guide for tacking and gathering. For the shirt on page 44 you will need seven dots, each 1 cm/$1/2$ in apart, in three rows.

2 Leaving a length of thread free at each end of the row, tack along the marked dots on all the rows. Insert a small pin at the end of each row, vertically against the last stitch. Holding the other end of the thread taut, pull up the near end by each pin and wind any spare thread around the pin. Repeat until all the ends are wound around a pin. Make sure that you gather all three rows evenly.

3 Now start to work your embroidery in stem stitch. Working from left to right, make small, even-length stitches, with the thread emerging each time on the left side of the previous stitch, so that there is no gap between stitches.

Vintage dress patterns

Discover them in specialist online stores, on ebay, or at charity shops or car boot sales. If you plan to use one, it's wise to check that it has all its pieces before you start buying fabric. And read the instructions carefully as they may differ from modern dress patterns (for example, some very old patterns don't have the seam allowances marked, or even included in some cases, and expect you to calculate it yourself).

THE PERFECT PLACKET

1 Cut a straight strip of material twice the length of the opening.

2 With right side of the strip to the right side of the garment, and the edge of the strip to the edge of the opening, seam to the end of the opening.

3 Pull the opening apart until it is one long, straight line. Without breaking the thread, continue stitching the strip to the opening.

4 Keeping the opening in one straight line, turn half of the strip to the wrong side. Turn in the hem allowance. Press. Hem just above the running stitches.

5 With the two halves of the opening right sides together, stitch a line of back-stitching at the bottom of the opening.

Embroidery Tips

Prettify your little projects with some fancy needlework. I have chosen a few simple yet classic embroidery designs to start you off. Once you have made your project think about how you can use embroidery skills to personalize store-bought baby clothes. For example, you can use the charted cross-stitch letters in the ABC Jeanius Blocks project (see page 18) to monogram a cotton jersey onesie (all-in-one suit) or add a personal message.

NEEDLE AND THREAD

You will need a large-eyed crewel or embroidery needle, rather than a standard sewing 'sharp' needle. Embroidery thread is available as single or stranded (up to six single thin strands twisted together), and in matt, pearl or lustrous finished cotton, rayon or silk.

HOW TO WORK

Working from left to right, begin with a small double-stitch to secure the thread. To finish off, take the needle through to the wrong side of the fabric. Thread the needle through the loops at the back of the last few stitches, until you feel it is safely held, then cut the loose end as close as you can to the stitches.

LAZY DAISIES

Such a summery stitch, Steps 1 to 3 will form a single petal or leaf. Repeat, working in a circle, to make a daisy.

1 Bring the needle through the wrong side at the inner (centre) end of a flower petal.
2 Holding the thread with your left thumb, put the needle back into the fabric where it came out and then bring it out to the right side of the fabric, at the outer end of the petal.
3 Still holding down the thread loop you have formed under the needle, pull the needle through, drawing up the thread until the loop lies loosely on the surface. Hold the loop down at its outer end by taking a tiny stitch across it.

FRENCH KNOT

A neat little whorl, this is an ideal stitch to represent the decorative centres of flowers or animal eyes. Vary the size of the knot by increasing or decreasing the number of twists in Step 2.

1 Bring the needle through from the wrong side of the fabric.
2 Twist the thread three times around the

Cheat's embroidery The blue
and white cotton lawn
machine-embroidered fabric
on the left would be a good
choice for the Heirloom Gown
project on page 36. The hand-
embroidered bib on the right
and the machine-quilted shoes
are vintage pieces.

needle, holding the free part of the thread
above the twisted part.

3 Still holding the thread, return the
needle to the wrong side of the fabric as
close as possible to where it emerged.

CROSS-STITCH

As the name says, it's a cross, rather like
the multiplication sign. It has multiple
uses. As well as lettering – see the
Jeanius ABC Blocks (see page 18) –
cross-stitch is also a good stitch to use
for border designs on household linens,
and for charted pictures.

1 Make two equal-length slanting stitches
laid over each other at right angles, to
form a multiplication cross.

2 To work a row of stitches, it is quicker
to work the single slants all in the same
direction and then return down the row,
before crossing them with the reverse
slanting stitches.

WHIPPED RUNNING STITCH

You can create straight or curved outlines,
or striped effects (see Lazy Daisy Pinafore,
page 82) with this laced running-stitch.

1 Working in your chosen colour, with
even spaces in between, sew a length of
small running-stitches.

2 Taking care not to pull the thread too
tightly, wrap a second thread in a
matching or contrasting colour through
the running-stitches. Stay on the right
side of the material and do not go through
to the reverse except at the beginning
and end of a row, or when you are
starting a fresh thread.

Vintage Knitting Know-How

Knitting matinée jackets or bootees for a baby shower used to be virtually compulsory for last century's housewives. Today, friends of the mother-to-be choose to take up their needles as a calming, creative respite from a busy day at work. If you are new to knitting you will find plenty of books and classes to guide you at your local yarn store.

Babies grow very fast and if you have a special occasion in mind you'll need to plan ahead to make sure you can finish the piece in time. Unless you are an experienced knitter or have plenty of time on your hands, choose a simple, quick-to-knit project.

You can knit up the smaller, plain version of the Candy Cane Christmas Stocking (see page 108) in a flash. Start it on Christmas Eve morning and you should finish in time for Rudolph and Santa to reach your chimney that night. This design is so easy it could be a great project for an older child to knit for a younger sibling (though you might like to give them more than a day to complete the task, to prevent tears at bedtime). For the hot summer months, the sunsuit is a breeze: if your trip is going to be a long one, take up your needles at the start of your journey and you may even have finished when you reach the beach.

KNITTING NEEDLE CONVERSION CHART		
Metric (mm)	Old UK	US
2	14	0
2.25	13	1
2.5	-	-
2.75	12	2
3	11	-
3.25	10	3
3.5	-	4
3.75	9	5
4	8	6
4.5	7	7
5	6	8
5.5	5	9
6	4	10
6.5	3	10.5
7	2	-
7.5	1	-
8	0	11
9	00	13
10	000	15

Using old needles To find out the size of unmarked vintage needles, like these plastic ones, first track down an old needle gauge, similar to the vintage one shown left, then use the conversion chart on the facing page to find the modern size.

NEEDLES

I have a big collection of vintage needles in coloured plastic and aluminium, and enjoy picking a colour to co-ordinate or contrast with my yarn – it all adds to the pleasure of knitting. Of the modern needles, bamboo ones are my current favourites as they are warmer to the touch than metal, yet the yarn still slips easily over them. Vintage needles came in a range of different sizes to today's European and American makes and were often unmarked. The chart on the left will help you to match today's needles to any old patterns you find – or your old needles to modern instructions.

CHOOSING YARN

Pure wools and silks are soft and natural, but may not be washable – though some are. Check the instructions on the ball band carefully, and if you are making the item as a gift consider whether the parent is likely to hand-wash it before you choose a yarn that needs special care. It is helpful to add a handwritten label to your parcel, with the washing instructions from the ball band.

Babies have sensitive skin and some are allergic to wool, so if the parents-to-be have allergies, you should consider using cotton, bamboo, acrylic or other itch-free yarns.

Pattern Templates

I have included the shaped pieces as scaled pattern diagrams for you to enlarge. Other pieces are simple squares or rectangles and measurements are provided on the project pages for you to use.

SIZING AND SCALE

Because of the size of the book, pattern pieces have been reduced to fit the page. Instructions on the page tell you what percentage reduction they are so that you can set your copier to scale up the pattern. You will need to use A3 paper for most patterns. Dress and shirt patterns are given in three sizes: select the coloured outline that matches your child's age. The inner outline is the smallest size, while the outer is the largest. For information on age measurements refer to the chart below.

SEAM ALLOWANCES

Pattern pieces don't include a seam allowance: add your desired amount. Originally, sewers would include generous allowances, with room to let the garment out, but today we usually prefer to start afresh. I would suggest 3 cm/1¼ in allowance, unless your fabric is likely to fray, or you wish to stitch a French seam, when 5 cm/2 in allowance is preferable.

All fabric amounts are based on an average 90 cm-/36 in-wide plain fabric. You may need to allow extra fabric to match patterns.

AGE MEASUREMENTS

Age	1 month	12 months	2 years	3 years	4 years	5 years
Height	56 cm	80 cm	92 cm	98 cm	104 cm	110 cm
	22 in	31 in	36 in	39 in	40 in	43 in
Chest	48 cm	50 cm	52 cm	54 cm	56 cm	58 cm
	19 in	19 in	20 in	21 in	22 in	23 in
Waist	37 cm	46 cm	48 cm	50 cm	52 cm	54 cm
	14 in	18 in	19 in	19 in	20 in	21 in
Hip	40 cm	52.5 cm	56 cm	58 cm	62 cm	64 cm
	15 in	21 in	22 in	23 in	24 in	25 in
Inside Leg	18 cm	19 cm	36 cm	40 cm	44 cm	47 cm
	7 in	8 in	14 in	15 in	17 in	18 in

CANDY CANE CHRISTMAS STOCKING PATTERN CHART

Working in knit one, purl one rib, follow this chart for the patterned section of the design. Find full project details on page 108.

Key
- ■ Red yarn
- □ White yarn

SKINNY MONKEY

Find project details on page 22.
These patterns are 15% of the full size, so set your copier accordingly.

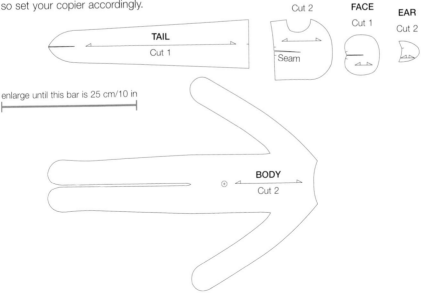

HEAD
Cut 2

FACE
Cut 1

EAR
Cut 2

Seam

TAIL
Cut 1

enlarge until this bar is 25 cm/10 in

BODY
Cut 2

LITTLE BOY BLUE SHIRT

Choose a lightweight cotton or silk shirting. As a guide for smocking gathers, mark out 3 rows of dots spaced 1 cm/³⁄₈ in apart in the areas marked on the pattern pieces. Find project details on page 44.

These patterns are 15% of the full size, so set your copier accordingly.
Ages 3, 4 and 5

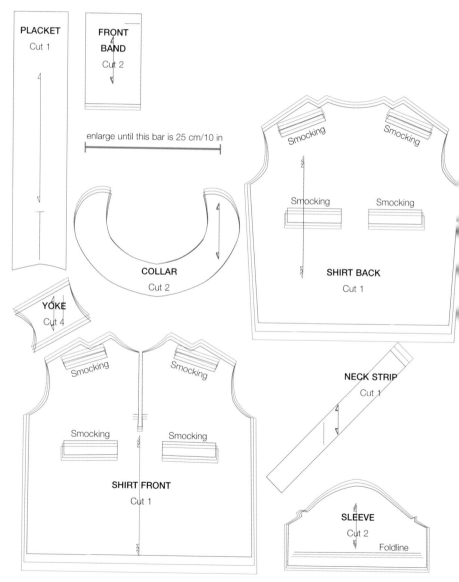

PLACKET
Cut 1

FRONT BAND
Cut 2

enlarge until this bar is 25 cm/10 in

COLLAR
Cut 2

Smocking Smocking

Smocking Smocking

SHIRT BACK
Cut 1

YOKE
Cut 4

Smocking Smocking

Smocking Smocking

SHIRT FRONT
Cut 1

NECK STRIP
Cut 1

SLEEVE
Cut 2
Foldline

SPOT SUNBONNET

Choose light or medium-weight cotton. With a medium-weight fabric you may choose to omit the lining. Find project details on page 64.

These patterns are 15% of the full size, so set your copier accordingly.

One size

PATTERN PIECES

Bonnet – cut 1 piece 55 cm/21½ in long and 22 cm/8½ in wide in main fabric, and 1 in lining fabric

Neck Binding Strip – cut 1 piece 26.5 cm/10 in long and 5 cm/2 in wide

Neck Cover – cut 1 piece 16 cm/6½ in wide and 35 cm/13 in long, fold and mark a centre back notch on one long edge

Brim – pattern provided

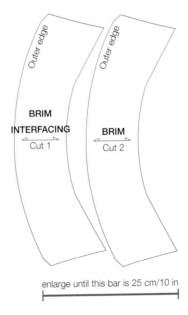

enlarge until this bar is 25 cm/10 in

RUFFLE BLOOMERS

Choose lightweight cotton fabric. Find project details on page 90.

These patterns are 15% of the full size, so set your copier accordingly.

Ages 3, 4 and 5

Front seam

BLOOMERS

Cut 2

Back seam

Casing line for ribbon placement

enlarge until this bar is 25 cm/10 in

DOWN-HOME OVERALLS

Choose a suitable cotton print – you can find reproductions of feedsack materials at quilting suppliers online or choose an appropriate mini-print such as a wild strawberry design. Find project details on page 56.

These patterns are 15% of the full size, so set your copier accordingly.

Ages 1,2 and 3

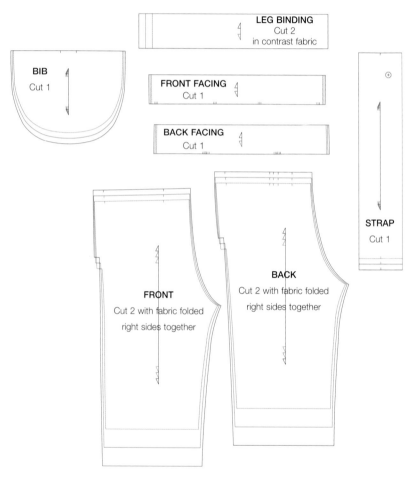

LEG BINDING
Cut 2
in contrast fabric

BIB
Cut 1

FRONT FACING
Cut 1

BACK FACING
Cut 1

STRAP
Cut 1

FRONT
Cut 2 with fabric folded
right sides together

BACK
Cut 2 with fabric folded
right sides together

enlarge until this bar is 25 cm/10 in

RICK-RACK YOKE DRESS

Choose a medium-weight cotton fabric – it needs to have enough body to hold the box pleats crisply. Find project details on page 60.

These patterns are 15% of the full size, so set your copier accordingly.
Ages 2, 3 and 4

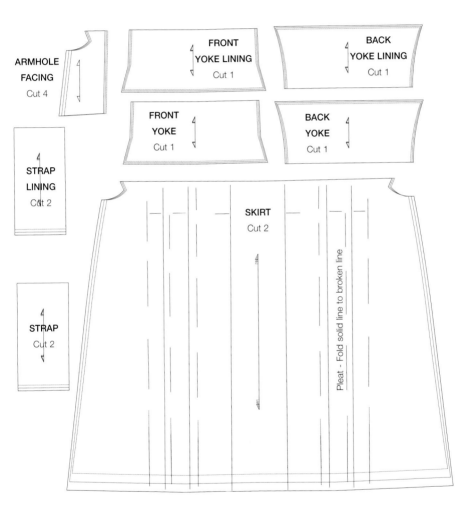

ARMHOLE
FACING
Cut 4

FRONT
YOKE LINING
Cut 1

BACK
YOKE LINING
Cut 1

STRAP
LINING
Cut 2

FRONT
YOKE
Cut 1

BACK
YOKE
Cut 1

SKIRT
Cut 2

STRAP
Cut 2

Pleat - Fold solid line to broken line

enlarge until this bar is 25 cm/10 in

COLLAR
Cut 2

Placement trim line

SLEEVE
Cut 2

BACK
Cut 1

FRONT
Cut 2 with fabric
folded right sides
together

SAILOR TOP

Choose lightweight cotton or linen. Find
project details on page 94.
These patterns are 15% of the full size,
so set your copier accordingly.
Ages 3, 4 and 5

enlarge until this bar is 25 cm/10 in

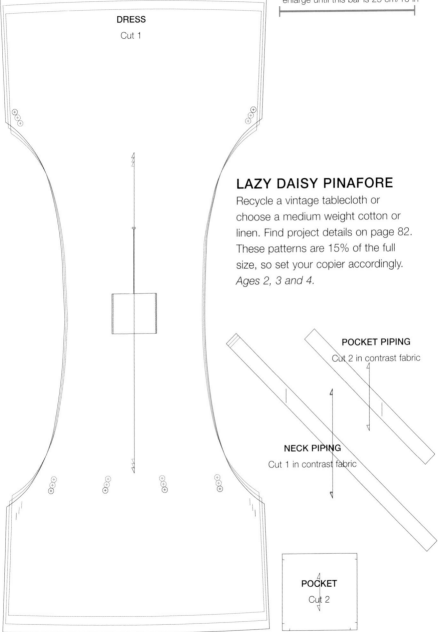

DRESS

Cut 1

LAZY DAISY PINAFORE

Recycle a vintage tablecloth or choose a medium weight cotton or linen. Find project details on page 82. These patterns are 15% of the full size, so set your copier accordingly. *Ages 2, 3 and 4.*

POCKET PIPING

Cut 2 in contrast fabric

NECK PIPING

Cut 1 in contrast fabric

POCKET

Cut 2

RUFFLE DRESS

Choose lightweight cotton or silk. Find
project details on page 86.
These patterns are 15% of the full size,
so set your copier accordingly.
Ages 3, 4 and 5

enlarge until this bar is 25 cm/10 in

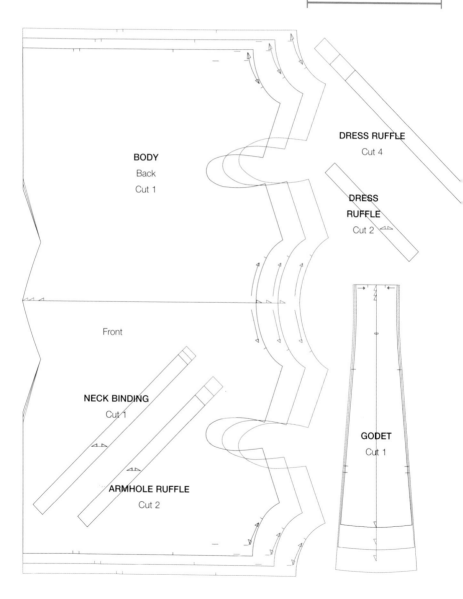

BODY

Back

Cut 1

Front

DRESS RUFFLE

Cut 4

DRESS
RUFFLE

Cut 2

NECK BINDING

Cut 1

GODET

Cut 1

ARMHOLE RUFFLE

Cut 2

DUCK LAUNDRY BAG

Find project details on page 104.
These patterns are 15% of the full size,
so set your copier accordingly.

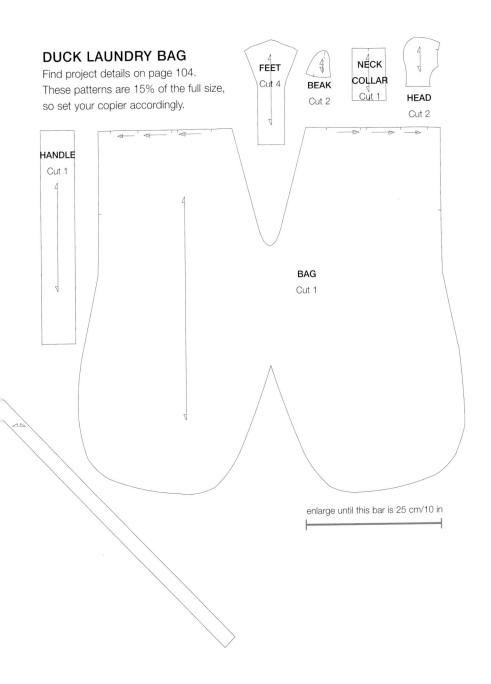

FEET
Cut 4

BEAK
Cut 2

NECK COLLAR
Cut 1

HEAD
Cut 2

HANDLE
Cut 1

BAG
Cut 1

enlarge until this bar is 25 cm/10 in

Useful Addresses

VINTAGE PATTERNS

www.acmenotions.com
Currently only shipping to the USA, with a large selection of vintage sewing patterns and vintage sewing and craft supplies.

www.grandmashouse.ws
US-based Grandma's House sells vintage, discontinued, uncut, new and used sewing patterns, hot-iron transfers, sewing and needlecraft books, needlework supplies, decorative painting books, vintage aprons, handkerchiefs, linens and other treasures.

www.misshelene.com
Miss Helene's sells vintage sewing patterns from the 1920s through to the 1980s, as well as a selection of newer, discontinued patterns.

www.momspatterns.com
Florida-based online seller.

www.oldpatterns.com
Large selection of patterns from 1920 onwards, including sewing, knitting and crochet.

www.patternrescue.com
They source missing pattern pieces and swap and recycle complete patterns.

www.sovintagepatterns.com
A selection of patterns from 1900 onwards.

www.vpll.org
The Vintage Pattern Lending Library is home to a growing collection of over 3,000 antique sewing and needlework patterns, vintage fashion publications, and other related historic print materials from the 1840s

through the 1950s, from the United States and abroad. They offer digital reproductions of many of the patterns in their collection for purchase or loan.

www.yesterknits.com
Based in Scotland, this is said to be the largest collection of vintage knitting patterns in the world. 250,000 individual designs are available, plus around 50,000 crochet patterns as copies.

FABRIC

www.buttonberry.com
Online store for fabrics, including vintage repro yardage.

www.cathkidston.co.uk
Cath Kidston
Cath Kidston vintage-style fabrics.

www.clothhouse.com
The Cloth House
47 Berwick Street, Soho, London W1F 8SJ

www.dalstonmillfabrics.co.uk
Dalston Mills Fabrics
69-73 Ridley Road, Dalston, London E8 2NP

www.gonetoearth.co.uk
Gone to Earth
12 Hill House Gardens
Stanwick Northants NN9 6QH

www.liberty.co.uk
Liberty
Regent Street, London W1B 5AH

www.macculloch-wallis.co.uk
MacCulloch and Wallis
25-26 Dering Street London W1S 1AT

www.nerybethcrafts.co.uk
Nerybeth Fabrics & Craft
Online fabric store.

www.reprodepot.com
Reproduction and hard-to-find Japanese
print fabrics.

www.vintagefabricmarket.co.uk
Online fabric store.

YARN
www.iknit.org.uk
Iknit London
106 Lower Marsh, Waterloo, London
SE1 7AB
My favourite knitting store.

www.knitrowan.co.uk
Rowan Yarn
Available from various outlets.

BUTTONS
www.buttonemporium.com

www.thebuttonqueen.co.uk
The Button Queen
15 Marylebone Lane, London W1V 2NF

www.button-shop.com
USA-based online store.

www.thebuttonshop.co.uk
The Button Shop
87 Green Street, Forest Gate, London
E7 8JF

GENERAL

www.beeinspired.co.uk
UK-based, craft supplies for busy bees.

www.corsetsandcrinolines.com
Vintage clothing and furniture.

www.etsy.com
Etsy
Craft items, including vintage-style designs
plus vintage fabrics and original patterns.

www.hobbyworld.co.uk

www.johnlewis.com

www.louiseloves.co.uk
Charmingly pretty shabby-chic items.

www.lulusvintage.com
US online vintage store.

www.nostalgiagames.net
Nostalgia Games
Traditional toys and games.

www.singermachines.co.uk

www.specialistauctions.com
Born Too Late Vintage
Look for Born Too Late items on this
auction site.

www.vintagesewing.info

www.vintage-toybox.co.uk
Vintage Toybox
Your childhood revisited.

Vintage Sewing Reference Library, Inc.
Offers free online access to public domain
sewing books.

www.vintagewallpaperonline.com
Gundry Lane, Bridport, Dorset

Index

Acknowledgements

THE AUTHOR AND FIL ROUGE PRESS WOULD LIKE TO THANK

The team: Janis Utton, Jo Godfrey Wood and Robin Lever for their hard work and good humour. Emily Hedges and Hannah Boyd for additional assistance. Victoria at MacCulloch and Wallis and Gemma at Rowan for their help and generous support. Amanda Kavenagh, Jan Nixon, Andy Piccos, Susan Smith and Helen Vallis for their help in making up some of the items for photography. Jonathan More, Lily More, Peter More, Emma Sergeant, Hannah Sergeant and Sarah Toogood for help and inspiration. James Mitchell, Chris Herbert and Andy Harris for professional advice.

PROJECT CREDITS

The knitting patterns for the bootees, sunsuit, shawl and striped sweater were adapted from vintage patterns originally published by companies owned by Coats & Clark. Coats & Clark group generously provided contemporary yarns for the adapted modern versions and for the Christmas stocking designed by the author. Original vintage patterns copyright Coats & Clark (various dates). Patterns are reproduced with the permission of Coats & Clark Inc. Original products and supplies for the patterns shown may no longer be available. Contemporary yarn details for the adapted versions are provided on the project pages.

The designs for the letters on the ABC blocks, and the monkey, heirloom gown, little boy's shirt, rosy purse, overalls, yoke dress, sunbonnet, pinafore, ruffle dress, bloomers, sailor top, splat mat and laundry bag were adapted from or inspired by 1920s and 1930s original documents or garments from the author's collection. The original documents and the original garment designs are in the public domain, but Fil Rouge Press holds copyright in the adapted versions, which must not be made for resale.

Love crafts? Crafters, keep updated on all exciting news from Collins & Brown. Email **lovecrafts@anovabooks.com** to register for free email alerts and author events.

Yarns were supplied by Rowan Yarn, Green Lane Mill, Holmfirth HD9 2BR or online at www.knitrrowan.com. Fabrics were supplied by MacCulloch and Wallis Ltd, 25 Dering Street, London W1S 1AT or online at www.macculloch-wallis.co.uk, who stock every kind of traditional and modern fabric, sewing aid and trimming.
Gingham cotton fabric 23248 (Achoo Stroller Quilt, Duck Laundry Bag)
Cotton moleskin 2512 (Skinny Monkey)
Sky-blue French embroidered cotton voile 2190 (detail on page 125; suggested fabric choice for Heirloom Gown)
Light blue silk dupion (Little Boy Blue Shirt)
Pale pink cotton poplin 2060 (Rosy Purse, Ruffle Bloomers)
White cotton poplin 2161 (Rosy Purse lining, Spotted Sunbonnet lining, Duck Laundry Bag head)
Cotton sateen ribbon 6046/25 col. 265 (laces for Snowdrop Bootees, Rosy Purse, Ruffle Bloomers)
Ribbon rosebuds 80153 (Rosy Purse, Ruffle Dress)
Printed cotton Strawberry Poplin 2805 (suggested fabric choice for Down-Home Overalls)
18mm jumbo Ric Rac 6050 (Rick-Rack Yoke Dress, Rick-Rack Splat Mat)
Embroidered cotton pique 2007 (Rick-Rack Yoke Dress)
Giant spotted cotton poplin 2163 (Spotted Sunbonnet)
White Irish linen (Lazy Daisy Pinafore)
Pale-pink dotted Swiss cotton Robia voile 2203C (Ruffle Dress, Ruffle Bloomers)
Royal blue cotton poplin 2060W (Sailor Top)
100 percent cotton 120mm grosgrain ribbon 14407/10
Ivory rayon Ottoman bias binding 198 (Sailor Top)

PICTURE CREDITS

All photographs by Robin Lever except for the photo frame: Photodisc/Alamy

All illustrations from original documents in the author's collection except for:
pages 13, 32 top, 35, 55, 72, 101: Mary Evans Picture Library; page 112: © Blue Lantern Studio/Corbis; page 70: Corbis.

Love crafts? Crafters…keep updated on all exciting craft news from Collins & Brown. Email **lovecrafts@anovabooks.com** to register for **free** email alerts on forthcoming titles and author events.